SEVEN KEY PRINCIPLES
FOR EFFECTIVE MINISTRY

SEVEN KEY PRINCIPLES FOR EFFECTIVE MINISTRY

Nurturing Thriving Churches
in a Postmodern Culture

David A. Harrell

Shepherd Press
Wapwallopen, Pennsylvania

© 2019 David A. Harrell

ISBN
Paper: 978-1-63342-130-1
epub: 978-1-63342-131-8
Kindle: 978-1-63342-132-5

Shepherd Press
P.O. Box 24
Wapwallopen, PA 18660

www.shepherdpress.com

Cover Design by www.greatwriting.org

Page Design and Typeset by **documen**, Wales. www.documen.co.uk

Printed in the United States of America

APPRECIATIONS

Dave Harrell outlines with unusual clarity the essential features of authentic church ministry. His textbook and ultimate source of authority is Scripture. His mentors are Christ and the apostles. His attitude is that of a shepherd, not a CEO. The result is a clear, compelling handbook for pastors and church leaders. Prepare to be instructed, encouraged, and powerfully motivated.

—John MacArthur, Pastor-Teacher, Grace Community Church; Chancellor, The Master's University and Seminary

The visible church today is overrun with men (and some women) who occupy positions of pastoral authority but are neither called nor qualified to lead the church. They take their cues on leadership from the corporate world, the entertainment industry, politicians, academicians, or other sources of worldly wisdom and human cleverness. The resulting philosophy of ministry is fundamentally pragmatic, not biblical. Pragmatists and showmen might be effective in putting on a spectacle that will draw a crowd, but what they are doing is not real ministry by any sound New Testament standard. They are not true shepherds of the flock of God. They are what Jesus was referring to when he spoke of "hirelings" in John 10:12-13. This helpful work by Dave Harrell succinctly summarizes the essential principles of authentic biblical ministry. It is an excellent corrective to the trends that have left so many postmodern evangelical churches spiritually weak and ineffectual.

—Phil Johnson, Executive Director, Grace to You

I have known and respected Dave Harrell for almost four decades. Because of his deep love for Christ and Scripture, it is no surprise to find his life experience as counselor, professor, pastor, and teacher poured out in this excellent work. I wish when I was a young pastor I would have learned these seven principles early on. This is a must read for every pastor and church leader and should be taught in every seminary.

—Tom Branson, Senior Pastor, Hanson Baptist Church, Hanson, Kentucky

In a time when experience, emotion, pragmatism, compromise, and even confusion sadly reign in many churches around the World, David Harrell rightly reminds us how God wants his shepherds to be devoted to ministry effectively. Instead of looking out for results, fame, or human success, this book rightly emphasizes that pastors around the globe should be devoted to shepherd the people of God his way and for his glory, following timeless biblical principles.

—David Robles, Pastor Iglesia Evangelica de Leon and President of Berea Seminary, Spain

In a world where words are many and distractions are vying for your attention, it is refreshing to have such a clear, direct, and powerful book like *Seven Key Principles For Effective Ministry*. David Harrell's gem is a book that you will want to pick up yearly, just to remind you of the ministry essentials and to encourage you to stay on track. As you read this book, you will feel like you are being mentored at the feet of an older, wise pastor. This will be a sure resource as we train pastors in Africa.

—Shannon Hurley, Founder, Sufficiency of Scripture Ministries, Uganda, Africa

We hear a lot today about ministerial burnout and there are a number of contributing factors. Dave Harrell addresses some of these factors in his book *Seven Key Principles for Effective Ministry*. If you are tempted to throw in the towel, or know someone who is, this book, written in the context of many years of pastoral experience and grounded in Scripture, will be useful to aid in staying the course.

—Joseph A. Pipa Jr., President, Greenville Presbyterian Theological Seminary, Taylors, South Carolina

There is nothing more stabilizing in ministry than sinking your roots very deep into the Scriptures in the midst of the howling winds of life. This is what David Harrell helps us to do. Consider the chapters of this book as seven roots that must sink very deeply if you are to bear God-glorifying fruit in and through the church in a culture that has gone adrift from the moorings of its Creator. You can never go wrong with God's wisdom! Here is a book worth reading and passing on to those just starting the journey of church leadership and ministry.

—Conrad Mbewe, Pastor, Kabwata Baptist Church, Lusaka, Zambia

DEDICATION

To my wife Nancy, for her Christlike example and loyal love—the most tangible expression of God's grace in my life. No husband could have a greater helpmate; no pastor could have a greater soulmate.

> *O magnify the LORD with me,*
> *And let us exalt His name together.*
>
> *Psalm 34:3*

ACKNOWLEDGMENTS

The idea for this book was a result of the Spirit's work in my heart when preaching through Paul's epistle to the Colossians, especially an exposition I did on chapter 1, verses 24-29 entitled *Seven Ruling Convictions of a Pastor's Heart*. Those few verses perfectly summarized a biblical paradigm for pastoral ministry that can be seen throughout the New Testament, and one that I had embraced since the beginning of my ministry.

Therefore, I also wish to thank the precious saints at Calvary Bible Church for their shared commitment to these key principles that emerge from Scripture; and, like the saints at Thessalonica, for their "work of faith and labor of love and steadfastness of hope in our Lord Jesus Christ in the presence of our God and Father" (1 Thessalonians 1:3).

I must also thank my dear friend and assistant, Pamela Ufen (a faithful and tireless servant along with her husband, Brian) for her copy editing in the very beginning stages of the process. I wish to also express my gratitude to my friend and fellow pastor, John Fast (Hilltop Bible Church, Murfreesboro, Tennessee) for exercising his spiritual discernment and theological acumen in critiquing the chapters during the initial editorial process prior to submitting it to a publisher.

A special thanks also goes to Jim Holmes, Acquisitions Editor at Shepherd Press, whose heart resonated with mine in the initial perusal and who recommended the book to Shepherd Press for consideration. Jim skillfully offered his wise input in the substantive editing process and continues to be a source of encouragement and inspiration.

And finally, I wish to express my appreciation to Tedd and Aaron Tripp at Shepherd Press for their willingness to collaborate with me in this publishing project, that in all things Christ might have the preeminence.

CONTENTS

PREFACE

I suppose entering the fourth quarter of life is similar to starting the fourth quarter of a football game. You know the clock will soon run out and you only have one final period of time to do your very best. This is where I find myself. Having spent the majority of my life serving Christ, first as a biblical counselor and professor, training and ministering to pastors and church leaders, then as the pastor of a start-up church in a rural suburb of Nashville, Tennessee (where I have now served for over two decades), I am now happy to be entering my fourth quarter.

Like every pastor, I hope to finish well. To use a worn-out sports cliché, "I hope to leave it all on the field!" In the end, I pray that I will be able to say with the apostle Paul, "I have fought the good fight, I have finished the course, I have kept the faith" (2 Tim. 4:7). And it is in this spirit that I have been compelled to write this book.

While every believer can benefit, this book is primarily for pastors, seminarians considering pastoral ministry, and church leaders who find themselves swimming against the current of a postmodern culture. It is written from the perspective of one who knows what it is to start a church with a handful of people and watch God grow it spiritually and numerically, against all odds.

I am also acutely aware of the challenges pastors face, especially the unique dynamics of smaller churches that make up the vast majority of evangelical churches around the world. I have spent much of my life caring for pastors: hearing their stories, sharing their pain, comforting their sorrows, confronting their sin, and encouraging them to stand firm, come what may. Through it all, I have learned much about myself, about pastoral ministry, about the church, and about the power of the Word of God to transform lives. I have also learned much about the diabolical schemes of the enemy to deceive, distract, divide, discourage, and destroy pastors and churches.

As in every period of redemptive history since the birth of the church at Pentecost, there have been troubling dispensations of compromise that have plagued the church. While the specifics may vary, in every situation the rise and fall of faithfulness in the church has been dependent upon *pastors*, men whom God has commissioned to speak on his behalf and shepherd his flock. When they have failed, the church has followed suit. But when they have stood firm in the faith, the church has flourished, not only surviving in the midst of great opposition, but also thriving as a result of it.

We now live in a postmodern age that poses many unique threats to the evangelical church. Many pastors admit they are in crisis because of this. Evangelicalism—once defined by its commitment to doctrines and practices of the Protestant Reformation—has now become an amorphous spiritual movement whose only connection to the historic Christian faith is what is written on the doctrinal statement of individual churches: a document most church members have never read and nor could they explain. Christianity today is being forced to embrace *experience* over *truth*. In fact, the concepts of *absolute* or *moral truth* are now rejected in our postmodern culture with its prevailing attitude of skepticism, subjectivism, and relativism. We live in a world where all viewpoints—no matter how absurd and contradictory—must be considered equally valid. Whether it is politics or religion, *emotion* has now replaced *reason*.

Unfortunately, most evangelicals believe the most effective means to reach this postmodern world for Christ is for the church to become more attractive and relevant to the culture. It must reinvent itself, adjust its gospel message, be less dogmatic, more therapeutic, tolerant, and entertaining. It must pander to the culture, take up its social causes, even conform to it, but never oppose it.

Others will argue, as I do in this book, that such a position is totally foreign to Scripture and therefore mitigates the power and blessing of God. Moreover, because God is not even remotely like us, it is foolish to try to make him part of us. His nature and attributes are infinitely beyond our ability to even imagine. His greatness and holiness are outside the bounds of our thoughts and ways. Therefore, he cannot be adapted to fit into our world—a world he has gone to such great lengths to save us out of and will one day destroy.

Though hideously offensive to the culture, God is concerned with only one thing: *his glory*, which is revealed most vividly in the person and work of his beloved Son, the Lord Jesus Christ, who died vicariously to save sinners. Because of this, his church is to be singularly focused on the gospel and his promise to save all who turn from sin and trust in Christ as Savior and Lord.

Furthermore, by its very nature the church is radically different from anything in culture. It is an outpost of a celestial kingdom the world cannot comprehend. It is made up of alien people whose citizenship is in heaven—people who have received a Word from another realm and who long to leave this earth at God's appointed time. So when Christians meet together to worship, they do so because an unfathomably glorious God has summoned them to *worship* him and *hear* from him, making their worship services an *otherworld* experience—a gathering where God speaks through the stammering lips of divinely appointed men, and where sacraments are administered in remembrance of Christ, keeping his worshippers in a state of breathless adoration.

In light of this biblical worldview, instead of reinventing the church to make it relevant, I will argue that we must recapture the essence of the New Testament church whose spiritual authenticity can be seen most clearly in the Protestant church of the Reformation.

But how do we do this, practically? What does this mean for pastors and church leaders? What was Paul's philosophy of ministry that unleashed the power of God in his gospel witness and made him so incredibly successful in planting churches? How did he guard his heart and avoid moral and doctrinal compromise in a world that was constantly trying to either seduce him or kill him? How did he not only *survive*, but also *thrive* in gospel ministry, despite such violent satanic opposition?

These are the kinds of questions Paul himself answered, especially in his testimony recorded in Colossians 1:24-29:

Now I rejoice in my sufferings for your sake, and in my flesh I do my share on behalf of His body, which is the church, in filling up what is lacking in Christ's afflictions. Of this church I was made a minister according to the stewardship from God bestowed on me for your benefit, so that I might fully carry out the preaching of the word of God, that is, the mystery which has been hidden from the past ages and generations, but has now been manifested to His saints, to whom God willed to make known what is the riches of the glory of this mystery among the Gentiles, which is Christ in you, the hope of glory. We proclaim Him, admonishing every man and teaching every man with all wisdom, so that we may present every man complete in Christ. For this purpose also I labor, striving according to His power, which mightily works within me.

The purpose of this book is to examine the life and ministry of the apostle Paul primarily (but not exclusively) through the lens of this passage of Scripture. From it will emerge *seven key principles* that informed his decisions, calmed his fears, and soothed his sorrows—principles every pastor and church leader can take to heart, seven divine mandates that must guide our ministry as they did his. Paul was:

1. Consumed with God's Glory
2. Content with His Suffering
3. Convinced of His Calling
4. Controlled by One Message
5. Confident with One Method
6. Committed to One End
7. Confirmed by One Power

Given the worldly influence of postmodernism upon the evangelical church that has greatly diminished its gospel impact on the culture, pastors and churches can gain biblical clarity and comfort by examining these convictions that guided the apostle Paul. It is my prayer that these principles will strengthen and encourage every faithful servant of Christ willing to engage in the battle for the gospel with courage, thoughtfulness, and love.

David Harrell

CHAPTER 1

KEY PRINCIPLE ONE: CONSUMED WITH GOD'S GLORY

"Whether, then, you eat or drink or whatever you do, do all to the glory of God."

1 Corinthians 10:31

Every faithful pastor and dedicated church leader will experience seasons of sorrow and betrayal. This should be no surprise, knowing we serve our Master who was "despised and forsaken of men, a man of sorrows acquainted with grief" (Isa. 53:3). Early on in my ministry there were times when I asked myself, "Why am I doing this?" "Am I really doing what God wants me to do and am I doing it the way he wants it done?" There were times when I literally wept over situations that were so deeply discouraging that I despaired of life itself.

While the etiology of depression can be multifaceted, the inevitable difficulties associated with pastoral ministry can be a contributing factor, a challenge for the most physically and spiritually robust pastor. In the early days of Charles Spurgeon's ministry, the pain of slander and scorn was so great that he was tempted to quit. His wife Susannah would often hide the morning newspaper to protect him from further insults. He described his melancholy this way: "The iron bolt which so mysteriously fastens the door of hope and holds our spirits in a gloomy prison, needs a heavenly hand to push it back."[1]

If you're in pastoral ministry, you know the feeling. You know what it is to exhaust yourself with the rigors of ministry, to pour your life into those over whom God has given you charge, and then something happens in the church that leaves you speechless, helpless, and tempted to throw in the towel. Although we can all find comfort in knowing God is up to something in our life during those crucibles of grace, we still struggle with fear and sometimes a lack of motivation. Most pastors I have counseled or know personally as friends will admit this.

What I have discovered from experience, and more importantly from Scripture, is that we need something more than knowing "God causes all things to work together for good" (Rom. 8:28)—even more than knowing "the testing of [our] faith produces endurance" (James 1:3), as true and wonderful as those promises are. We need something so awe-inspiring, so motivating, that nothing can prevent us from getting back up when we get knocked down—something that will always inspire us to grab our sword and get back in the fight.

What we need is *a zeal for the glory of God*—a zeal that can only come from *a soul-captivating and sin-destroying vision of the majesty of God.* I am not referring to an actual vision like the six visions seen by Paul and recorded in Acts. Nor am I speaking of the supposed revelatory visions or dreams common in the Charismatic movement. Rather, I am referring to a life-dominating obsession with the intrinsic glory of God—seeing him as he has revealed himself in creation and Scripture, and calling all people to worship King Jesus who has been given all authority over heaven and earth (Matt. 28:17-20) and granted "an everlasting dominion which will not pass away" (Dan. 7:14).

In Ephesians 1 the apostle Paul addresses God's commitment to his own glory in salvation in what might be considered a magnificent hymn of praise. Speaking of our spiritual blessings in Christ, he reminds us how the Father

> *chose us in Him before the foundation of the world, that we would be holy and blameless before Him. In love He predestined us to adoption as sons through Jesus Christ to himself, according to the kind intention of His will,* **to the praise of the glory of His grace***, which He freely bestowed on us in the Beloved.*
>
> *(Eph. 1:4-6, emphasis mine)*

We must remain forever preoccupied with these profound truths, allowing them to evoke within us a reverential awe that will naturally result in a wholehearted devotion to his glory in all that we do, come what may. This is consistent with Jesus' command: "Let your light shine before men in such a way that they may see your good works, and glorify your Father who is in heaven" (Matt. 5:16). This is what it means to have a *zeal for the glory of God.* We must have a soul-consuming infatuation with the manifestation of the character of God in his works, his Word, and his people—an awe of God so profound that our heart will sing its own version of David's paean of praise:

> *I will extol You, my God, O King, and I will bless Your name forever and ever.*
>
> *Every day I will bless You, and I will praise Your*

name forever and ever.

*Great is the Lord, and highly to be praised, and
His greatness is unsearchable.*

*One generation shall praise Your works to
another, and shall declare Your mighty acts. On
the glorious splendor of Your majesty and on
Your wonderful works, I will meditate.*

(Ps. 145:1-5)

Having a preoccupation with the unfathomable glory and greatness of God is not a suggestion; it is a command! Speaking through his inspired psalmist, God adjures the whole of his creation saying, "Let all the earth fear the Lord; let all the inhabitants of the world stand in awe of Him" (Psalm 33:8). This kind of perspective puts everything else in life, both good and bad, in its proper perspective. Nothing in life compares to the incomprehensible perfections of our Creator and Redeemer whose glory we will one day share.

Does this characterize the passion of your heart? Do you "Glory in His holy name" (1 Chron. 16:10)? Hopefully we can all share Solomon's doxology of adoration:

*Blessed be the LORD God, the God of Israel, Who
alone works wonders.*

*And blessed be His glorious name forever; and
may the whole earth be filled with His glory.
Amen, and Amen.*

(Ps. 72:18-19)

A GLIMPSE OF GOD'S GLORY

Perhaps a short primer on the transcendent majesty of God would be helpful to fan the embers of our passion into full flame once again. Between the foolish preoccupations of our flesh and the godless distractions of the world, it is easy for this blaze to be extinguished.

The Old Testament Hebrew term for glory (*kabod*) comes

from a root that means "heavy" or "weighty." It carried the idea of the heaviness of something and was therefore a measure of its worth or value. For example, we might say something is "worth its weight in gold." Therefore the term is often used in a figurative sense to suggest the remarkable worthiness or intrinsic value of a person.

In the New Testament, the term for glory is *doxa,* from which we get our English word *doxology.* In the Hellenic culture, *doxa* was used to express the high opinion people had toward someone based upon his character or achievements. In the Septuagint it was used to express the shining radiance of the glory of God, which was pictured in the Old Testament as the very essence of his nature manifested in his created universe through both natural and special revelation (Psalm 19).

The apostle Paul also made it clear in his epistles that *all God is and does speaks of his intrinsic glory* (e.g., Eph. 1:6; 3:16; Col. 1:11) and especially his invasion into his material universe. This is seen most clearly in the incarnation of Christ, which the apostle John described in these words: "And the Word became flesh, and dwelt among us, and we saw His glory, glory as of the only begotten from the Father, full of grace and truth" (John 1:14).

It was a passion for this very glory that occupied the Savior's heart on the eve of his crucifixion. In his High Priestly Prayer, he prayed that his disciples would see the essential nature of God in his actions and be awestruck by the magnificence of the Lord their God in his work of redemption. He prayed: "Father, the hour has come; glorify Your Son, that the Son may glorify You.... And now, glorify Me together with Yourself, Father.... And the glory which You have given Me I have given to them; that they may be one, just as We are one" (John 17:1, 5, 22).

To be sure, Jesus' glory was veiled when he took on human flesh. But it partially broke through that veil when the effulgence of his glory emanated from him on the Mount of Transfiguration (Luke 9:29-31). We see something similar when the angry mob came to arrest him in the garden. He asked them, "Whom do you seek?" They answered him, "Jesus the Nazarene." He said to them, "I am He." When therefore He said to them, "I am He," they drew back, and fell to the ground" (John 18:5-6). Just by speaking the covenant name of God, "I am" (*Ego eimi*), his glory broke through the veil and sent his adversaries to the ground! There the Lord of glory merely uttered the title he used to describe himself in John 8:58 where he told the unbelieving Jews, "before Abraham was born, I am"—referring to himself in the present continuous tense which speaks of his self-existence; he *has* always and *will* always exist. There has never been a time when he did not exist. Here we see that God's glory and his name are synonymous.

Moses warned the Israelites "to do all the words of this law that are written in this book, that you may fear this glorious and awesome name, the LORD your God" (Deut. 28:58). In the Psalter, he is referred to as the "King of glory" (Ps. 24:8, 9, 10), and the "God of glory" (Ps. 29:3). For this reason the Psalmist exclaims: "Not to us, O Lord, not to us, but to Your name give glory" (Ps. 115:1). God is jealous of his name because he is jealous of his glory. In his model of prayer, Jesus commands us to pray, "Our Father who is in heaven, hallowed be Your name" (Matt. 6:9), a passionate petition (not a declaration) for God to make his name hallowed (sanctified). We are to pray that he will cause his name to be treated with utmost holiness that he might be feared, obeyed, worshiped, and glorified (Lev. 10:3).

He even gave us a terrifying vision of his glory when he manifested it visibly in the pillar of cloud and fire (his *Shekinah* presence) that once covered Mount Sinai, then led the Israelites in their wilderness pilgrimage to the Promised Land. What a beautiful picture of his redeeming grace that we proclaim as ministers of the gospel of Christ; the One who is the very personification of the glory of God (2 Cor. 4:5-6); "the radiance of His glory and the exact representation of His nature" (Heb. 1:3).

And in every demonstration of God's glory we clearly behold his *holiness*, the all-encompassing attribute of his infinite perfection, purity, and power. It is therefore our zeal for God's glory that unleashes the power of the Holy Spirit within us, causing our lives to redound to his glory and our souls to be flooded with the inexpressible joy of his presence. For this reason alone, as pastors we must have a *zeal for the glory of God*; more than all others we must possess *a soul-captivating and sin-destroying vision of the majesty of God*. I fear, however, that this is not the norm in our evangelical culture. Many worship what

David Wells describes as a "weightless" God:

It is one of the defining marks of our time that God is now weightless. I do not mean by this that he is ethereal but rather that he has become unimportant. He rests upon the world so inconsequentially as not to be noticeable. He has lost his saliency for human life. Those who assure the pollsters of their belief in God's existence may nonetheless consider him less interesting than television, his commands less authoritative than their appetites for affluence and influence, his judgment no more awe-inspiring than the evening news, and his truth less compelling than the advertisers' sweet fog of flattery and lies. That is weightlessness.[2]

As ministers, we have been called and gifted to proclaim the gospel of God and live lives that emanate his glory. We are to "Sing to the Lord, bless His name; proclaim good tidings of His salvation from day to day. Tell of His glory among the nations, His wonderful deeds among all the peoples. For great is the Lord and greatly to be praised; He is to be feared above all gods" (Ps. 96:2-4). We are to emulate the kind of worship on earth that the angels and saints who have gone on before us offer in heaven (Rev. 5:12-14).

This is the reason we exist! The Westminster Shorter Catechism had it right: "Man's chief end is to glorify God and enjoy him forever" (Ps. 86; Isa. 60:21; Rom. 11:36; 1 Cor. 6:20, 10:31; Rev. 4:11). Is this the passion of your heart?

In his book *The Forgotten Spurgeon*, Iain Murray described how a zealous preoccupation with the glory of God unleashed the Spirit's power in Spurgeon's ministry saying,

A solemn sense of responsibility was not the impelling motive of his preaching, he was constrained by something higher than the call of duty—

> *Yet if I might make some reserve,*
> *And duty did not call,*
> *I love my God with zeal so great*
> *That I would give Him all.*

These words take us to the heart of Spurgeon's preaching.
He loved to proclaim "the glory of God in the face of Jesus
Christ." Christ—he was the "glorious, all-absorbing topic"
of Spurgeon's ministry and that Name turned his pulpit
labours into "a bath in the waters of Paradise."[3]

We see the importance of this kind of reverence and the all-consuming wonder of God's glory all through Scripture, especially in Paul's epistles. But somehow I missed it in my early days as a pastor. Maybe you have, too. Allow me to remind you of the context of Paul's letter to the Colossians. From it we will see how his zeal for the glory of God motivated his every word and deed.

THE MESS AT COLOSSAE

Like all churches confused about the person and work of Christ, the first-century church at Colossae was in something of a mess. It was founded by Epaphras, who was probably saved on a visit to Ephesus where he encountered the apostle Paul, who labored there for three years. The Jewish and Gentile composition of the church resulted in a bizarre blending of culture, religion, and philosophy that Satan used to create some very appealing—yet deadly—heresies.

The Gentiles were heavily influenced by Greek philosophy. They believed the soul was a divine spark of spirit imprisoned in the body—the philosophic seed that led to various forms of Gnosticism. For them, the spirit was good but matter was evil, so they scoffed at the idea of the incarnation of Christ. They could not fathom a God who would take on a human body and become a God/Man, and neither could they comprehend Christ being the very embodiment of truth. They believed transcendent spiritual knowledge was only available to a select few. Only highly enlightened initiates could ever ascend to the loftiest level of spirituality. We see elements of this kind of mysticism in virtually every false religion today, from Roman Catholicism to Buddhism.

The Jewish believers at Colossae, however, infected the church with something different. They brought with them certain elements of asceticism (practicing strict self-denial as a spiritual discipline) and legalism (salvation plus circumcision, the practice of feasts and festivals, ceremonial rituals, dietary laws, Sabbaths, etc.), along with the worship of angels and their own version of mystical experiences. Poor Epaphras! Jewish *asceticism, legalism,* and pagan *mysticism*—his church had become a seething cauldron of deadly deceptions. Given this, he traveled all the way to Rome (Col. 4:12-13) to seek counsel from the apostle Paul who was in prison there, and by God's grace, his counsel is available to all of us as well.

PAUL'S ZEAL FOR GOD'S GLORY

The heresies in the church at Colossae were like cancer cells that never die but continue to grow and form new abnormal cells that invade other tissues. For this reason, in response to Epaphras, Paul wrote the epistle to the Colossians from prison, warning them, "See to it that no one takes you captive through philosophy and empty deception, according to the tradition of men, according to the elementary principles of the world, rather than according to Christ" (Col. 2:8).

I find Paul's response here, as well as the entirety of his epistle, to be driven by the most fundamental of all doctrines, and therefore the primary motivation of his life and ministry: *a zeal for the glory of God as seen in the person and work of Jesus Christ.*

From the outset he asserted the supremacy of Christ over all his creation saying, "For by Him all things were created, *both* in the heavens and on earth, visible and invisible, whether thrones or dominions or rulers or authorities—all things have been created through Him *and for Him*" (Col 1:16, emphasis mine). Paul was enthralled by the reality that God created all things to put his glory on display forever! Though he languished in a Roman dungeon, he was eager to defend the ineffable grandeur of God's glory, which he had witnessed firsthand on the road to Damascus when confronted by the Lord Jesus Christ himself. At the very beginning of his conversion and ministry he was given *a vision of the glory of God resulting in a zeal for his glory.*

God also allowed Paul to witness the stunning wonder of his majesty when he was "caught up into paradise" (2 Cor. 12:3) where he heard and saw things so inconceivable "they cannot be told, which man may not utter" (v. 4). Paul's experiences help explain his passion in revealing the deity of Christ in Colossians—a passion every pastor must share. Knowing that God is most glorified by his saving grace through Christ (John 17:5), we, like Paul, desire that people see the glory of our King and serve him in "His kingdom ... which will not be destroyed" (Dan. 7:14). The transcendent holiness of his person and the greatness of his works humble us to the core. This is what ignites our zeal for evangelism. Paul put it this way:

> For we do not preach ourselves but Christ Jesus as Lord, and ourselves as your bondservants for Jesus' sake. For God, who said, "Light shall shine out of darkness," is the One who has shone in our hearts to give the light of the knowledge of the glory of God in the face of Christ.
>
> (2 Cor. 4:5-7)

We see this theme throughout his letter to the Colossians. After Paul has expressed his gratitude for their faith (1:3-8) and prayed for their spiritual wisdom, understanding, and growth energized by an ever-increasing knowledge of God (vv. 9-14), the remainder of the chapter reads like an extended doxology of praise concerning the exalted Christ. You get the sense that his pen cannot keep pace with his heart as it explodes with passionate and contagious praise.

Paul was consumed with the glory of God—the most essential ruling conviction of a pastor's heart. He makes it clear that the greatness of God's glory does not merely exist outside of a believer, but also *inside*. This was "the mystery which [had] been hidden from the past ages and generations, but has now been manifested to His saints" (v. 26)—"Christ in you, the hope of glory" (v. 27). This was an exhilarating truth that motivated him to labor and strive (v. 29).

And it is thrilling to know that because of the indwelling Spirit's work of sanctification, we are gradually being transformed into the likeness of Christ. But we do not merely *reflect* his glory; it *radiates* from within us. For this reason Paul says, "We all, with unveiled face, beholding as in a mirror the glory of the Lord, are being transformed into the same image from glory to glory, just as by the Spirit of the Lord" (2 Cor. 3:18). What a magnificent reality!

His unyielding focus on the glory of God—especially as it relates to the believer's exalted calling—comes through loud and clear in his admonition to the saints when he says:

> *Therefore if you have been raised up with Christ, keep seeking the things above, where Christ is, seated at the right hand of God. Set your mind on the things above, not on the things that are on earth. For you have died and your life is hidden with Christ in God. When Christ, who is our life, is revealed, then you also will be revealed with Him in glory.*
>
> *(Col. 3:1-5)*

Paul understood what it was to live on a higher plane—to transcend the temporal by focusing on the eternal. He knew there was nothing on this earth that can bring lasting joy and satisfaction, despite the lusts of the flesh that tell us otherwise. He knew that God had placed within us an insatiable hunger to know him and a thirst that can only be quenched by his presence. Every twice-born saint will say with the psalmist, "As the deer pants for the water brooks, so my soul pants for You, O God" (Ps. 42:2).

Soli Deo gloria was the bedrock affirmation of the Reformation. The eternal purpose of God's plan of redemption is to reconcile sinners to himself and restore us to a place where our lives redound to his glory. This only occurs through a decisive commitment to personal righteousness and holiness (Eph. 1:4; 2 Cor. 11:2, 3) anchored in the bedrock of divine revelation. Holiness and truth are two sides of the same coin. If our zeal for God is not in accordance with truth, then it will be for a god we have created in accordance with our own lusts, desires, prejudices, and theological traditions. It is impossible to have a zeal for the glory of God apart from a zeal for the truth he has revealed to us in his inspired Word, a reality that is sorely missing in evangelicalism today.

The Jews had zeal, but without knowledge, and many Christians have knowledge without a genuine love for God and his truth. Most churches simply will not tolerate sound doctrine. Their commitment to the truth is determined by their worldly interests, not from a love for the truth and the glory of God.

But it is our personal pursuit of holiness based upon Scripture that is at the very heart of Paul's exhortation when he said, "Whether, then, you eat or drink or whatever you do, do all to the glory of God" (1 Cor. 10:31). Believers who have no commitment to personal holiness and righteousness based upon the truth of God's Word will never be overwhelmed by the unfathomable greatness and power of God. Their lives will never redound to his glory. Instead, they will be greatly limited in their effectiveness in serving Christ—especially if they are pastors! We of all people must be devoted to these fundamentals of the faith. Only then will we be overwhelmed by the glory of God that now resides in us.

Think about it: in a mystery beyond our capacity to understand, God *redeemed* us that he might *inhabit* us. We exist in him: "Our life is hidden with Christ in God" (Col. 3:3). For this reason Paul says, "If the Spirit of Him who raised Jesus from the dead dwells in you, He who raised Christ from the dead will also give life to your mortal bodies through His Spirit who dwells in you" (Rom. 8:11). In light of this, we can consider the glory dwelling within us as being like a spiritual nuclear warhead awaiting detonation. The supernatural abilities we possess because of our union with Christ are unimaginable, yet we are often tempted to function in our flesh rather than believing we, "can do all things"—that is, suffer all things, endure all things, persevere in all things, trust in him in all things—"through Him who strengthens [us]" (Phil. 4:13).

We can therefore understand how Paul could exclaim, "Now to Him who is able to do far more abundantly beyond all that we ask or think, according to the power that works within us, to Him be the glory in the church and in Christ Jesus to all generations forever and ever. Amen." (Eph. 3:20-21). Can there be any greater encouragement to serve Christ without fear or compromise? The greatest motive to serve Christ must be a sincere love for him and his Word because they are inseparable. This translates into a pastoral ministry that is unwilling to compromise in a world that increasingly demands just that.

The more we refuse to cave in to the culture, the more we

will find ourselves standing alone in ministry. We will be like Joshua and Caleb, who came perilously close to being stoned for going against the temper of the people. We will be like Micaiah, who stood alone against the united opinion of 400 prophets. We will be like Shadrach, Meshach, and Abednego, who, out of all the Jews exiled to Babylon, refused to bow to the golden image. We will be like Luther, who refused to compromise with Rome; we will join the ranks of all the martyrs burned by Bloody Mary for refusing to affirm the real presence in the bread and wine. But because of Christ who strengthens us, we will persevere with power and joy.

Because of Christ's atoning work and the pouring forth of his Spirit upon us, we also share in the blessings of the transcendent awesomeness of God. The apostle Paul described this by contrasting the glory of God that was neglected by Israel with the surpassing glory of God that must be wholeheartedly embraced as a result of the New Covenant.

> *But if the ministry of death, in letters engraved on stones, came with glory, so that the sons of Israel could not look intently at the face of Moses because of the glory of his face, fading as it was, how will the ministry of the Spirit fail to be even more with glory? For if the ministry of condemnation has glory, much more does the ministry of righteousness abound in glory. For indeed what had glory, in this case has no glory because of the glory that surpasses it. For if that which fades away was with glory, much more that which remains is in glory.*
>
> *(2 Cor. 3:7-11)*

The glory that reflected off the face of Moses gradually faded away, symbolizing the fading glory of the old covenant. But the surpassing glory of the new covenant that permanently replaced the old *will never fade away*, having been completed forever by Christ's sacrificial death on the cross: "For by one offering He has perfected for all time those who are sanctified" (Heb. 10:14). To use the vivid imagery of the old covenant tabernacle, the glory of God that once hovered between the cherubim over the mercy seat and above the Ark of the Covenant now resides in the redeemed, making each one of us a temple of the Holy Spirit (1 Cor. 6:19). This truth alone should animate the heart of every pastor to ever-increasing heights of personal purity and passion for Christ, that he might have the preeminence in all things!

THE IMPLICATIONS OF THE RESURRECTION

We must also remember that the *implications of the resurrection and glorification of Jesus Christ* exceed the importance and power of all other events in history. Only the actual creation of the universe rivals it, because within the resurrection body of Jesus Christ existed the supernatural power source of eternal life and God's everlasting kingdom. Paul prayed for the Ephesians, that they would know "what is the immeasurable greatness of His power in us who believe, according to the working of His great might which He accomplished in Christ when He raised Him from the dead and made Him sit at His right hand in the heavenly places" (Eph. 1:19-20). This is a prayer we should pray for our congregation and for ourselves.

Contained within the resurrection body of Christ was the supernatural seed of resurrection glory for all whom the Father had given him, the power source of the universe, "Christ in you, the hope of glory" (Col. 1:27). We have been supernaturally united to the Creator and Sustainer of God's everlasting kingdom. And think how this relates to us: "Christ has been raised from the dead, the first-fruits of those who have fallen asleep. For as by a man came death, by a man has come also the resurrection of the dead. For as in Adam all die, so also in Christ shall all be made alive" (1 Cor. 15:20-22).

In Christ we have been given a new kind of existence. Remember, his body was made perfect, no longer subject to weakness or death, but able to live eternally. He "put on immortality," therefore, like his resurrection body, ours will also be raised "imperishable ... in glory ... in power ... a spiritual body" (1 Cor. 15:42-44). We will be given a body like Christ's, one fit for heaven, no longer subject to sickness and death or shame because of sin, no more frailty in temptation, no more limits to the time-space sphere in which we currently exist. Within the resurrection body of Christ was the infinite power of the self-existent, pre-existent, uncreated Creator of the universe who spoke all things into existence and upholds all things by the word of his power—a force infinitely more powerful than anything man can create or even conceive. And to think that one day we will behold him (1 John 3:2), dwelling in a body that will in many ways look like ours, yet from it will emanate the effulgence of his celestial majesty, the resplendent light of his glory blazing forth with more brilliance than the sun.

Indeed, Christ is the "first fruits"—a precise sample of the coming harvest, which means our resurrection bodies will in many ways be like his, minus the incommunicable attributes that are his alone. No wonder Paul, despite being physically beleaguered, was so excited in his response to the Colossians. *He was consumed with the glory of God!* He understood that he was united to the risen Christ, the source of eternal life for all who believe in the crucified and resurrected Son of God.

The Scottish preacher, William Still described this in his inimitable style when he said:

> *He is the embryo of all that one day will exist outside of hell. All that does not belong to Him in His resurrection body, and issues not from Him, will be burned up one day. Only that which is transformed by His coming power and glory will remain. The potential of that New Christ that stood before Mary at the first so that she mistook Him for the gardener, is the source of all that will survive the original creation when it is burned up and reconstituted. And it is the Holy Spirit sent from Him, belonging to Him, and enshrining all the virtues of His victories over all evil, who dwells in your poor heart and mine.[4]*

What a precious comfort this should be to every child of God. And what a motivation it should be to every faithful pastor who labors in the Word, wars against the world, shepherds his sheep, and runs off the wolves. Because of this we can say with Paul:

> *Therefore we do not lose heart, but though our outer man is decaying, yet our inner man is*

being renewed day by day. For momentary, light
affliction is producing for us an eternal weight of
glory far beyond all comparison, while we look
not at the things which are seen, but at the things
which are not seen; for the things which are seen
are temporal, but the things which are not seen
are eternal.

(2 Cor. 4:16-18)

GOD'S GLORY IN GOSPEL PREACHING

Epaphras was losing heart. Who wouldn't, in light of all the chaos in his home church? He needed encouragement, and the mixed-up believers needed a good dose of truth, especially as it related to the preeminence of Christ. This is where effective ministry must begin—with a consuming passion for the glory of God that shines most brightly in the "gospel of the glory of Christ" (2 Cor. 4:4). Like the saints at Corinth, Paul wanted them to see "the light of the knowledge of the glory of God in the face of Christ" (2 Cor. 4:6). He wanted them to manifest this gospel-producing glory like the Thessalonians, of whom he said, "God from the beginning chose you for salvation through sanctification by the Spirit and belief in the truth, to which He called you by our gospel, *for the obtaining of the glory of our Lord Jesus Christ*" (2 Thess. 2:13-14, emphasis mine).

Now, practically speaking, no pastor will be able to fearlessly and faithfully preach the gospel in all its purity and power unless he has an unshakeable zeal for God's glory. Without this, he will subtly, perhaps unwittingly, develop *a zeal for his own glory.*

o   He will promote himself rather than God, forgetting that God will share his glory with no other (Isa. 42:8).

o   He will seek the applause of men rather than God, forgetting that, "We have this treasure in earthen vessels, that the surpassing greatness of the power may be of God and not from ourselves" (2 Cor. 4:7).

o   He will be more concerned with personal image and pleasure than personal holiness and self-denial (2 Cor. 7:1; Luke 9:23).

○ He will be more concerned with methods than motives, forgetting Paul's testimony to the Corinthians when he said, "I was with you in weakness and in fear and in much trembling" (1 Cor. 2:3).

○ He will confuse emotion with worship in Spirit and truth (John 4:24).

○ He will preach the latest theories of psychology and sociology rather than the inspired, inerrant, infallible, authoritative, all-sufficient Word of God (2 Tim. 4:2).

○ He will labor to understand the contemporary culture rather than endeavoring to understand Scripture (2 Tim. 2:15).

○ He will grow increasingly skilled in theatrics and manipulative techniques to get people to "make a decision for Christ" because he fails to understand that we do not bring people to Christ; we bring Christ to people! And when he is rightly proclaimed, God himself will breathe spiritual life into the spiritually dead, awaken sinners to faith, and in his great mercy cause them to be born again (Rom. 10:17).

For this reason Paul went on to say that his "message and [his] preaching were not in persuasive words of wisdom, but in demonstration of the Spirit and of power, that [their] faith should not rest on the wisdom of men, but on the power of God" (1 Cor. 2:4-5). But sadly, this is not what we see in many evangelical pulpits today. Instead, we witness self-promoting pastors preaching a watered-down version of the gospel designed to appeal to the spiritually dead and the most immature saints in the congregation. To be sure, preaching "a different gospel" that "perverts the gospel of Christ" (Gal. 1:6-7) will definitely fill worship centers. But it will also deceive sinners, infect the church with the spirit of the age, rob God of his glory, and bring about divine retribution. For this reason, Paul thundered against those who preach a foreign gospel, saying, "Let him be accursed.... Let him be accursed" (vv. 8-9). Cursed is the man who dares to alter or adulterate the way God has chosen to reveal his glory to a lost and dying world through his gospel.

What has been lost in most gospel preaching today is God's purpose in saving sinners. It stops at forgiveness and ignores and even scorns holiness. It diminishes the miracle of regeneration by ignoring that God implants a new principle of life in every true believer. This new creature is not stillborn; true holiness is not a forced and learned habit that does nothing. It is a new principle of life. No sooner is this principle implanted than the true child of God seeks to live for the glory of God with all his might. The more he grows, and the more light he has to see by, the more he will see sin and the world in their true colors. The seed the Spirit sows in the soul does not lie dormant, but quickly sprouts and shows that it is alive by the fruit it bears.

All living things naturally grow, and part of that growth for a believer will include a soul-captivating wonder of God's intrinsic glory—a glory that even resides within him—and when he anticipates the full completion of the glory that awaits him, nothing else in life matters. His heart will long to see the perfections of God manifested through his works, his Word, and his people. He will live with an exhilarating awareness that one day he will actually partake of the very glory he adores. He will be the rare man who is truly "looking for the blessed hope and the appearing of the glory of our great God and Savior, Christ Jesus" (Titus 2:13). The hope of seeing and sharing in the glory of God in Christ will fill his heart with praise and cause him to say with Paul, "We exult in hope of the glory of God" (Rom. 5:2). Everything he does will be motivated by his desire to promote the awe and adoration of his coming Savior and King, and the exhilaration of knowing that he will eventually "stand in the presence of His glory blameless with great joy" (Jude 24).

Paul David Tripp summarized how this practically translates into our life and ministry:

> *The spiritual warfare of ministry is all about awe. The big ongoing battle in ministry is not a battle of time, finances, leadership, or strategy. The big battle is a battle of awe. The fear of man that grips so many ministry people and produces in them timidity and compromise is an awe problem. Sleep interrupted by anxiety about the finances of the church is an awe problem. Being too ruled and controlled by your own plan for the church is an awe problem. Being too conscious of how people see and*

respond to you is an awe problem. Settling for ministry mediocrity is an awe problem. Being too dominant and controlling in your ministry is an awe problem. Being self-righteous and defensive is an awe problem. Living in isolation, afraid of being known, is an awe problem. Arrogant theological "always-rightism" is an awe problem. Only awe of God can produce that balance between humility and boldness that marks all successful ministries.[5]

An awe problem must therefore first be understood as a self problem. We tend to love self too much and Christ too little.

THE EXAMPLE OF ISAIAH

Every pastor needs a good dose of what motivated Isaiah to continue to preach to a people whom, for the most part, God had judicially hardened and promised to judge. Have you ever thought about that? How could Isaiah endure ridicule and rejection his whole life in service to God? What motivated him to persevere in ministry in the face of such overwhelming opposition? The answer is as simple as it is profound: *he had a soul-terrifying, sin-destroying vision of the glory of God!*

After he witnessed the majesty and mercy of God, he was never the same. He "saw the Lord sitting on a throne, lofty and exalted, with the train of His robe filling the temple" (Isa. 6:1). He saw the seraphim hovering around the throne of God to do his bidding, calling out to one another, "'Holy, Holy, Holy, is the LORD of hosts, the whole earth is full of His glory.' And the foundations of the thresholds trembled at the voice of him who called out, while the temple was filling with smoke" (vv. 3-4). As he stood in the presence of the consuming fire of divine holiness with his sinfulness fully exposed, his heart erupted in confession saying: "Woe is me, for I am ruined! Because I am a man of unclean lips, and I live among a people of unclean lips; for my eyes have seen the King, the LORD of hosts" (v. 5). Then after taking the initiative to cleanse the prophet of his sin, the Lord said, "Whom shall I send, and who will go for Us?" to which Isaiah responded (v. 8), "Here am I. Send me!"

Isaiah's response, subsequent ministry, and martyrdom were all motivated not only by God's *mercy*, but also by his *majesty!*

He was driven by something even greater than reciprocal love. He had *a zeal for the glory of God*, a consuming passion to live in light of, and to one day stand again in the presence of, the ineffable glory of the living God.

SUFFERING AND GLORY

In the early days of my ministry when I experienced the lowest depths of sorrow, and grace seemed like a tiny spark about to be extinguished, the Lord graciously showed me how desperately I needed Isaiah's motivation. I needed to be, as Paul said, "strengthened with all power, according to his glorious might, for all endurance and patience with joy" (Col. 1:11, ESV). I needed that driving force underscored by the triumphant motto of the Reformers: *Soli Deo Gloria*. Perhaps this resonates in your heart as well.

This is also what motivated the battle-scarred apostle Paul who said, "Whatever you do in word or deed, do all in the name of the Lord Jesus, giving thanks through Him to God the Father" (Col. 3:14). And again in 1 Corinthians 10:31 he says, "Whether, then, you eat or drink or whatever you do, do all to the glory of God." This speaks of a glory we currently *share* and will one day *manifest* in full. Rejoicing in this astounding promise, Paul says, "For this reason I endure all things for the sake of those who are chosen, that they also may obtain the salvation which is in Christ Jesus and with it eternal glory" (2 Tim. 2:10).

This must be our passion as pastors. Whenever we lose sight of this, we not only find ourselves struggling to "suffer hardship ... as good soldiers of Christ Jesus" (2 Tim. 2:3), but we redirect our attention from *motives* to *methods*, foolishly believing that some new approach in ministry will alleviate our pain, or we seek after some fleeting pleasure. We also forget that our participation in the suffering of Christ is the very pathway to glorification. Paul put it this way:

> *The Spirit Himself testifies with our spirit that*
> *we are children of God, and if children, heirs*
> *also, heirs of God and fellow heirs with Christ, if*
> *indeed we suffer with Him so that we may also*
> *be glorified with Him. For I consider that the*

> *sufferings of this present time are not worthy to
> be compared with the glory that is to be revealed
> to us.*
>
> *(Rom. 8:16-18)*

But too often as pastors we want relief more than blessing. When this happens, we go on a fool's errand that robs God of his glory and subtly shifts it onto ourselves. As a result, our life and ministry begin to center around people's approval rather than God's. We may become more popular with other people and our church may increase in number, but it will not grow in a burning desire for the glory of God demonstrated by a membership that has a passion "to walk in a manner worthy of the calling with which [they] have been called" (Eph. 4:1).

FINAL WORDS

The glory of God awaits its full expression in the redeemed; and this is to be the center of gravity around which our lives and ministry must orbit. Why would Isaiah labor as a hated prophet of the Most High, knowing that virtually no one would heed his warnings? Why would Peter serve Christ faithfully for three decades, knowing all along it was God's will for him to be crucified at the end of his life (John 21:18)? Why would Paul endure unimaginable persecution and physical torture for the cause of Christ? The answer is this: *they were utterly captivated by the knowledge of the glory of God in the face of Christ!*

When the prophet Agabus told Paul what awaited him in Jerusalem, Paul's response was, "I am ready." God had so prepared, determined, and fixed Paul's will for the greatest of sufferings, "even to die" rather than compromise one hairsbreadth of God's truth to save himself. He counted his life as not dear to himself, and if we are to walk in his example, as he instructed Timothy and all who would come after him, then we must come to the same place. Are we ready? Most never count the cost, and most are lacking in a passionate yearning to see the glory of God put on display, regardless the cost.

As ministers of the gospel, may we do all we can to regain and maintain this life-dominating vision, that we might manifest a contagious zeal for the glory of God in our lives and ministry—*the first key principle for effective ministry.* May we live every moment of our lives with a passionate anticipation of that day when "the glory of the Lord will be revealed, and all flesh will see *it* together; for the mouth of the Lord has spoken" (Isa. 40:5). And when others see our unfailing commitment to the majesty of Christ in our lives, and hear it in our words, may they also say, *Soli Deo Gloria!*

PRAISE, MY SOUL, THE KING OF HEAVEN

Praise, my soul, the King of Heaven,
To his feet your tribute bring.
Ransomed, healed, restored, forgiven,
Evermore his praises sing.
Alleluia! Alleluia!
Praise the everlasting King!

Praise him for his grace and favor
To our fathers in distress;
Praise him, still the same as ever,
Slow to chide, and swift to bless.
Alleluia! Alleluia!
Glorious in his faithfulness!

Frail as summer's flow'r we flourish;
Blows the wind and it is gone.
But, while mortals rise and perish,
God endures unchanging on.
Alleluia! Alleluia!
Praise the high Eternal One!

Angels in the height, adore him;
You behold him face to face.
Saints triumphant, bow before him,
Gathered in from every race.
Alleluia! Alleluia!
Praise with us the God of grace!

Henry F. Lyte (1793–1847)

CHAPTER 2

KEY PRINCIPLE TWO:
CONTENT WITH HIS SUFFERING

"Now I rejoice in my sufferings for your sake, and in my flesh I do my share on behalf of His body, which is the church, in filling up what is lacking in Christ's afflictions."

Colossians 1:24

Like no other apostle, Paul suffered greatly because of his unwavering devotion to the gospel and his love for Christ and his church. At his conversion, the Lord spoke to him through a man named Ananias concerning "how much he must suffer for My name's sake" (Acts 9:16). To be sure, "All who desire to live godly in Christ Jesus will be persecuted" (2 Tim. 3:12). This truth bears elaboration.

As pastors and church leaders, we must understand that it is not a *form* of godliness the world maligns and hates, but the *power* of godliness. The world can live at peace with any number of forms of godliness. Satan does not care if the world thinks someone is a good Christian as long as he knows that person is still his slave. How can any form of godliness offend the devil when he is its inventor? Rather, it is sincere godliness and holiness in its simplicity and purity, founded on and guided by the pure Word of God, that the world hates. It is true gospel godliness that incites the anger and malice of Satan and his followers because it exposes the unfruitful deeds of darkness for what they really are.

We must also note that the kind of godliness to which Paul refers is "in Christ Jesus" (2 Tim. 3:12). There are all sorts of counterfeit forms of holiness and godliness in the world. If there is one thing the devil has learned it is that out-and-out persecution usually strengthens the church, but it is unholiness, worldliness, and compromise that ruin it. Notice, even the desire to live in a godly manner is enough to incite the hatred of the world, because then we no longer desire to seek the approval of the world, or to run in the same excess of dissipation as they do, so they malign us. The world hates Christians because we are not of the world. Our values and gospel message are offensive to Satan's diabolical world system (which is self-worship and self-glorification) designed to thwart the purposes of God and thus diminish his glory. Like the inhabitants of Babel, the world says, "let us make a name for ourselves" (Gen. 11:4).

Jesus said he had not come to bring peace to earth, but a sword (Matt. 10:34), and because the world hates him, they will also hate and persecute all who follow him (John 15:18, 20).

Jesus came to destroy the works of the devil, so the devil does all he can to incite his agents who disguise themselves as servants of righteousness to undermine the work of Christ by inventing all sorts of counterfeits and calling them by the same names. Because of this we must remain forever vigilant and discerning.

But it is also true that the inevitable suffering of God's people will extend beyond the opprobrium of the world. It will also include things like chronic illness, terminal disease, calamities, bereavement, poverty, heart-wrenching burdens, broken relationships, the horrors of war, and numerous other hardships God uses as a means of discipline which ultimately "yields the peaceful fruit of righteousness" (Heb. 12:11). There is a great difference between the sufferings that are the result of living in a sin-cursed world and are the effect of rejecting and rebelling against God's Word, and the suffering that is the result of being a Christian and desiring to live godly in Christ Jesus. One is common to all people, but the other is reserved only for true believers. One is cause for great repentance and/or patience, while the other is a cause for rejoicing, for "the Spirit of glory and of God rests upon you . . . if anyone suffers as a Christian, he is not to be ashamed, but is to glorify God in this name" (1 Peter 4:14-16).

Every faithful pastor can (and often will) experience these same things, and more—especially in his role as a shepherd. After describing the horrific forms of persecution he had endured from the world, Paul said, "Apart from such external things, there is the daily pressure on me *of* concern for all the churches" (2 Cor. 11:28). We can only imagine the many battles he faced and the interpersonal problems he had to deal with in the churches he planted and shepherded. In varying ways we experience the same. We can identify with Paul as we endeavor to bear up under the sheer weight of having to constantly "[b]e on guard for yourselves and for all the flock, among which the Holy Spirit has made you overseers, to shepherd the church of God which He purchased with His own blood" (Acts 20:28), and with Paul we can all say, "Who is adequate for these things?" (2 Cor. 2:16).

In fact, Scripture reveals a variety of unique forms of suffering that seem to be reserved for those God has called to shepherd his flock. From Moses' forty-year banishment in the wilderness to Paul's "thorn in the flesh," God uses special categories of suffering to accomplish his purposes in the lives of his shepherds. The goal of this chapter is to reflect upon these matters as a way of encouraging pastors and office-bearers to respond to suffering and indignities in ways that produce within them the soul-satisfying felt presence of God that inevitably results in adoring worship and Spirit empowerment, which, as we will see, is his ultimate desire.

A Warning to Potential Pastors

What I'm about to say is very true, very typical, and can be very discouraging. So before I say it, I think it is important to offer some real hope and encouragement to soften the blow. Many pastors, and I include myself, can wholeheartedly affirm the tremendous blessings of pastoral ministry. Although the pastorate is often overwhelming and never without heartache, for the most part it is far more *encouraging* than *discouraging*. My own journey has been filled with numerous battles, some with individuals under my care who were some of the most wicked people I have ever known. Out of the many pastors I have counseled and mentored over the last thirty years, I have yet to see an individual who has not been deeply wounded by one of his own elders (this has certainly been my experience as well). From Jezebel to Judas, Demas to Diotrophes, Ananias and Sapphira to Euodia and Syntyche, I've encountered them all. But I can say with utmost sincerity, the faithfulness and goodness of God has been a constant source of inexpressible joy resulting in much fruit in my life and in the lives of those I have had the privilege to shepherd. To be sure, my testimony can be echoed by countless others, and I sincerely hope it will be the shared testimony of those reading this book.

However, I must be frank: most churches are a disaster—train wrecks either waiting to happen or already derailed. Many have had *Ichabod* written across their entryway for years but they do not know it or refuse to admit it. Like Samson, "but he did not know that the LORD had departed from him" (Judg. 16:20). Every church will be home to both sheep and goats, both of which can be divisive and factious (1 Cor. 11:18-19), who are always causing trouble and blaming it on someone else. With the instability and volatility of nitroglycerin, they are ready to explode at the slightest bump of disagreement or wounded pride.

Most smaller churches are *family owned and operated*, controlled by a biblically undiscerning, theologically illiterate oligarchy with no intention of submitting to a godly shepherd, though they would deny it to the death. Even in larger churches, very few men in leadership meet the qualifications of an elder (1 Tim. 3:1-7; Titus 1:1-9) and most have no clue how to shepherd their flock. This is especially true in churches ruled by a single pastor or ruled by the congregation rather than a plurality of qualified elders (consistent with New Testament teaching).[6] In the absence of godly elders, churches governed by incompetent leaders or a "majority rules" democracy are notoriously factious and undiscerning. The preeminent preacher of The Great Awakening, George Whitefield, once stated, "As God can send a nation or people no greater blessing than to give them faithful, sincere, and upright ministers, so the greatest curse that God can possibly send upon a people in this world is to give them over to blind, unregenerate, carnal, lukewarm, and unskilled guides."[7]

It is also worth noting that the typical search committee (that some readers may encounter) is often made up of men and women from various groups within a church who are equally ill-equipped and undiscerning. It is like blind people trying to select someone who can see. When the blind lead the blind, both will fall into the ditch. They could be likened to well-meaning folks who went to various doctors on multiple occasions but then joined together to select the best brain surgeon to be chief of staff at the local hospital. The problem is, they don't know a cranium from a cerebellum or a scalpel from a suture. So the main criteria of the typical pastoral search committee will be defined by *personality* and *preaching style*. Regrettably, most do not have sufficient spiritual discernment and theological acumen to look beyond the superficial externals of a great interview and a well-rehearsed "trial sermon" that will most likely be the best sermon the candidate will ever preach and not be a representative sample of what they can expect long term.

Naturally the prospective pastor will be excited, but in most cases he will also be naïve. He will be like a sixteen-year-old boy at a used car lot preparing to buy his first car. He's so thrilled at the prospect of what he will look like behind the wheel that he fails to consider what's under the hood, not to mention the cost of insurance! That is where a wise father comes in real handy. Many pastors, especially new ones, are no different. I have seen it on multiple occasions. They are so thrilled at the prospect of what they will look like standing behind the pulpit they fail to consider what is really going on under the hood of the church. Because they really want the search committee to like them, they avoid asking the hard questions that might kill the deal— questions like:

- "How do you explain the short tenures of your previous pastors, and do you mind if I talk with them?"
- "What do you perceive to be the greatest spiritual weaknesses of the church?"
- "What are the greatest burdens of the leadership for the congregation, and what are they doing to address them?"
- "What kind of appetite does the church have for systematic, in-depth, expositional preaching, teaching, and application, and on what basis do you make your evaluation?"
- "Tell me about the prayer life of the church; does it reflect the principles set forth in Scripture?"
- "Can you describe and validate the church's commitment to evangelism and discipleship?"
- "Who offers biblical counseling to your people, and to what extent are you equipping your folks to facilitate biblical soul care?"
- "How do you handle church discipline?"

Furthermore, the fearful prospective pastor typically does not interview the leadership *personally* and *privately* to ascertain their spiritual maturity and their true (not merely stated) doctrinal positions. He does not ask them to explain how they would handle probable "hot button" issues related to things like divorce and remarriage, homosexuality, immodest dress, controversial personal preferences, and divisive doctrinal issues. He does not ask them to list the books they have been reading in the past year and perhaps the top five books that have had the most influence on their life. He does not ask them to list five pastors and/or theologians who have had the greatest impact on their lives. He does not ask them to describe what spiritual gift(s) *others would affirm in them* and how they are using them. And so on.

So at the end of the day, in most cases, neither the church nor the potential pastor really knows the other very well, but they decide to get married anyway. Then, after the honeymoon is over (usually about one year), the numerous underlying problems begin to surface, exposing the inadequacies and sinful proclivities of the congregation, the leadership, and the pastor himself. With expectations on both sides not being met, those keeping a record of wrongs begin to publish them. Little fires of gossip and slander blaze up in unexpected places, keeping the pastor on constant alert. His frustration and anger grows along with theirs. Even his clearly stated and previously agreed upon doctrinal positions are suddenly perceived to be divisive by some. Certain antagonists begin to emerge and form a coalition of opposition. Naturally, the pastor feels threatened. His family feels a growing sense of alienation. He fears his position is in jeopardy and starts forming his own opposition party, and so the war escalates.

This is the perfect scenario for Satan to do his mischief. This is how churches split. Eventually conflict becomes the center of gravity around which everything orbits. Biblical priorities like evangelism, equipping the saints, discipleship, shepherding, and the adoring worship of God are replaced by ungodly mayhem. Rather than loving and serving each other, the factions "bite and devour one another" (Gal. 5:15). People begin to leave the church. Friends become enemies and the pastor grows disillusioned and depressed. So he turns in his resignation, or he is fired.

Broken, bitter, and utterly exhausted, many leave the ministry—sometimes to save their marriage, and in some cases, to save their health. I've counseled men (and their wives) in this tragic condition more times than I wish to remember. Their stories are heart wrenching.

We see this illustrated in the average tenure for a Southern Baptist pastor, which is just over two years according to Thom Rainer, president of *LifeWay Christian Resources of the Southern Baptist Convention*. He makes this observation:

Though I found no singular reason for the third-year departure, I heard a number of common themes:

○ The honeymoon was over from the church's perspective. The church began seeing the imperfections in the pastor's ministry. Many brought concerns about those imperfections to the pastor.

○ The honeymoon was over from the pastor's perspective. Some of the promises made by those who first sought the pastor were unfulfilled. Some of the pastors indeed felt they were misled.

○ When a new pastor arrives, most church members have their own expectations of the pastor. But it is impossible to meet everyone's expectations. By the third year, some of the members become disillusioned and dissatisfied.

○ Typically by the third year, the church has a number of new members who arrived under the present pastor's tenure. Similarly, some of the members who preceded the pastor have died or moved away. The new members seem great in number to existing members. Some are threatened by these changes.

○ In any longer term relationship, that which seems quaint and charming can become irritating and frustrating. The pastor's quirks thus become the pastor's faults.

○ All relationships have seasons. None of them can remain on an emotional "high."[8]

To be sure, there are many other variables that can contribute to brief tenures and church splits, but those considerations are beyond my purpose here. My goal is simply to warn potential pastors of the hidden reefs they must navigate when considering pastoral ministry—dangers that will exist even in the very best of churches with the most qualified leaders. Remember, ministry is war! So don't be surprised when you take fire.

Many young men considering pastoral ministry are driven more by *romance* than *reality*. They fail to take into consideration that they will be shepherding people who have grown up in a culture that *demands autonomy and resents authority* and have therefore never truly been shepherded by a godly, gifted, fearless shepherd. Moreover, the lack of biblical discernment in evangelicalism today is staggering. Few know what it means to separate truth from error and "examine everything carefully" (1 Thess. 5:21).

Having been involved in crisis management with numerous churches and their leaders, it has been my unfortunate observation that most are too undiscerning to even know they're undiscerning. The light that is in them is darkness. They are unable to see how tradition, error, experience, and emotion have replaced the careful exegetical exposition of the Word that God uses to sanctify his people (John 17:17; 2 Tim. 4:4-5), and trying to explain these things can be like presenting the glory of the gospel to a dung beetle. Much of contemporary evangelicalism is mere "children, tossed to and fro by the waves and carried about by every wind of doctrine, by human cunning, by craftiness in deceitful schemes" (Eph. 4:14).

We see this, for example, in the steady stream of best-selling books that I have had to deal with over the course of my ministry—books like *This Present Darkness, The Prayer of Jabez, The Purpose Driven Life, 40 Days of Purpose, Your Best Life Now, Wild at Heart, The Shack, 90 Minutes in Heaven,* and *Jesus Calling,* to name a few—bewitching aberrations of the true gospel (Gal. 3:1) and of *Sola Scriptura.*

Combine all this with the *divisive, factious* people that God allows to exist in every church "in order that those who are approved may have become evident among you" (1 Cor. 11:19), and you can see how challenging pastoral ministry really is.

THE SOURCE AND PURPOSE OF OUR SUFFERING

While "the sufferings of Christ are ours in abundance" (2 Cor. 1:5) we can find relief when we contemplate the divine source and purpose of our sufferings, and this also informs a proper response.

Technically, this subject falls under the efforts of *theodicy:* the vindication of divine goodness and providence in view of the existence of evil. It is quite common for people to attempt to either *attack* or *rescue* the character of God for allowing evil to enter his perfect creation for reasons he never fully discloses. In fact, God makes no attempt to justify his actions; he is not subject to any human court. For this reason, our best efforts to explain him in this regard are woefully inadequate. However, Scripture does provide some general categories of thought that give us a basic understanding.

Said simply, God has made it clear in his Word that he is both *sovereign* and *omniscient*.

There is therefore nothing in our life he has not ordained to allow or does not understand completely, including our suffering. His sanctifying purposes are always at work. For this reason Paul exhorts us to "exult in our tribulations" (Rom. 5:3)—not merely to rejoice in spite of them or to resign ourselves to them and somehow choose to be happy; not even to rejoice in the midst of them, though that is important. What he is saying is that we are to exult *because* of our tribulations, *on account* of them! And he goes on to tell us why: "knowing that tribulation brings about perseverance; and perseverance, proven character; and proven character, hope; and hope does not disappoint, because the love of God has been poured out within our hearts through the Holy Spirit who was given to us" (Rom. 5:3-5). He obviously understood that God ordains our afflictions for our good and his glory.

In the fire of affliction, all we lose is our dross. If we remain faithful to his Word we can have the confidence to say with Job, "When He has tried me, I shall come forth as gold" (Job 23:10). Faith *must* be tested by fire (1 Peter 1:7). An untested faith is a dubious faith. An untried commitment is an unreliable commitment.

GOD'S SOVEREIGNTY AND OMNISCIENCE IN SUFFERING

As a pastor, it is comforting to know that God is fully in charge of all that happens. Nothing catches God by surprise, including our suffering.

With respect to his *sovereignty*, we must remember that he is the One who, declares "the end from the beginning, and from ancient times things which have not been done, saying, 'My purpose will be established, and I will accomplish all My good pleasure'" (Isa. 46:10). There is nothing a human being can do to escape his influence: "The mind of man plans his way, but the Lord directs his steps" (Prov. 16:9; cf. Jer. 10:23). Daniel described God as the One who "does according to His will in the host of heaven and among the inhabitants of earth; and no one can ward off His hand or say to Him, 'What have You done?'" (4:35; cf. Ps. 135:6). In these and many other verses God leaves no doubt that he reigns in absolute sovereignty over his creation as the One who "works all things after the counsel of His will" (Eph. 1:11). What a comforting truth!

Regarding his *omniscience*, "The Lord looks from heaven; He sees all the sons of men; from His dwelling place He looks out on all the inhabitants of the earth, He who fashions the hearts of them all, He who understands all their works" (Ps. 33:13-15). In utter awe, David described how God knew the minutest details of his life (Ps. 139:1-6). In Psalm 147 the Lord is praised as the One who heals the brokenhearted—the One who "counts the number of the stars and who gives names to all of them. Great is the Lord and abundant in strength; His understanding is infinite" (v. 4).

There is nothing a person can think or do that escapes his notice, "For the ways of a man are before the eyes of the Lord, and He watches all his paths" (Prov. 5:21). Indeed, "The eyes of the Lord are in every place, watching the evil and the good" (Prov. 15:3). "His understanding is inscrutable" (Isa. 40:28); "There is no creature hidden from His sight, but all things are open and laid bare to the eyes of Him with whom we have to do" (Heb. 4:13); "He knows everything" (1 John 3:19).

GOD'S GLORY IN SUFFERING

Saints through the ages have found great consolation in knowing that whatever the suffering, God is not only intimately aware of it, but he is also ultimately the *source* of it, even if it is the result of evil. We see that from the beginning *God ordained to allow evil to enter his perfect universe through the voluntary choices of moral creatures in order to dramatically display his glory through his holiness, wrath, mercy, grace, love, and power* (Romans 9). Although this is true, it is a supreme blasphemy to consider God the *author* or *cause* of sin. Because God is infinitely holy (Lev. 11:44-45), utterly bereft of any form of unrighteousness (Deut. 32:4; Ps. 92:15), he cannot act wickedly

(Job 34:10). Habakkuk said of the Lord, "Your eyes are too pure to approve evil, and You can not look on wickedness with favor" (Hab. 1:13). He cannot be tempted by evil or solicit anyone to do evil (James 1:13).

While our holy God is never the cause of sin, he does superintend its outworking through the willing, voluntary actions of moral creatures. This is evident in God's testimony of himself when he said, "I form the light, and create darkness: I make peace, and create evil: I the LORD do all these things" (Isa. 45:7 KJV). This would include not only the evil propensity in Satan and the angelic beings, but also the actual decree that they would eventually rebel.

John also tells us that "the devil has sinned from the beginning," referring to the first time he rebelled against God. But he went on to add, "the Son of God appeared for this purpose, to destroy the works of the devil" (1 John 3:8). This indicates that even the devil's diabolical works had to have been divinely ordained because Christ was "delivered up by the predetermined plan and foreknowledge of God" (Acts 2:23). Satan's original rebellion against God, his temptation of Eve in the garden, his temptation of Christ, his future empowerment of the Antichrist, his notorious opposition to the work of God, all had to have been known by an omniscient God who also ordained them by his uninfluenced will. To say otherwise would deny his right and claim to sovereignty, and would cause these texts to beg for relevance.

We can therefore conclude that God's elective, eternal purposes were decreed and set into motion before creation. This would include the Lord's incarnation and atoning work that defeated Satan, sin, and death. Here again we see that *he ordained to allow evil to enter his perfect universe through the voluntary choices of moral creatures in order to dramatically display his glory through his holiness, wrath, mercy, grace, love, and power.* Indeed, all of his elective purposes were ordained "from all eternity" (2 Tim. 1:9; Titus 1:2), literally, "before time began," which would by implication include his divine decree for Satan to rebel, Adam and Eve to sin, and, by imputation, all men to sin in Adam, thus requiring "the Lamb [to be] slain from the foundation of the world" (Rev. 13:8).

THE UNDERSTANDING OF OLD TESTAMENT SAINTS

That God brought about evil to accomplish his glorious purposes—including the evils we experience as pastors and church leaders—was well understood by his covenant people in the Old Testament. We see this in their repentance when in utmost contrition they cried out to God and said, "Why, O LORD, do You cause us to stray from Your ways and harden our heart from fearing You?" (Isa. 63:17; cf. 45:6-7). Likewise, the prophet Jeremiah lamented, "Is it not from the mouth of the Most High that both good and ill go forth?" (Lam. 3:38). Solomon reminds us that, "the LORD has made all things for Himself, even the wicked for the day of evil" (Prov. 16:4). Hannah praised God's sovereignty—even over evil—when she prayed, "The LORD kills and makes alive; He brings down to Sheol and raises up. The LORD makes poor and rich; He brings low, He also exalts" (1 Sam. 2:6-7).

Jeremiah understood that even in God's judgment of Judah, his grace, mercy, and compassion could still be seen, "For He does not afflict willingly or grieve the sons of men" (Lam. 3:33); nevertheless, it is God who is the ultimate source of it, so Jeremiah asks rhetorically, "Who is there who speaks and it comes to pass, unless the Lord has commanded it? Is it not from the mouth of the Most High that both good and ill go forth?" (Lam. 3:37-38). The prophet Amos also declared, "If a calamity occurs in a city has not the LORD done it?" (Amos 3:6).

We never know for sure what God may be up to when suffering as a result of evil afflicts us in some painful and unexpected way. We can never know God's secret will (Deut. 29:29); we can only submit to it, confident that it comes from the hand of a loving Father. We have trials because we need them, and we have no more of them than we are in need of. I'm sure Joseph was confused when his brothers captured him and sold him into slavery—a great example of God's providence orchestrating evil through the choices of sinful individuals.

Similarly, when Israel conquered the exceedingly wicked people of Canaan, in Joshua 11 we read, "Joshua waged war a long time with all these kings. . . . *For it was of the LORD to harden their hearts*, to meet Israel in battle in order that he might utterly destroy them, that they might receive no mercy, but that he might destroy them, just as the LORD had commanded Moses" (vv. 18-20, emphasis added).

God's sovereign rule over the affairs of men and women by indirectly bringing about sin through their choices is also evident in the account of the exodus when "The LORD said to Moses, 'When you go back to Egypt see that you perform before Pharaoh all the wonders which I have put in your power; but I will harden his heart so that he will not let the people go'" (Ex. 4:21). Then later God told Moses, "But I will harden Pharaoh's heart that I may multiply My signs and My wonders in the land of Egypt" (7:3; cf. 9:16; 14:17).

When God judged David for his sin, He also brought about evil through the willing actions of David's family. There we see God using sin to punish sin. We read of this in 1 Samuel: "Thus says the LORD, 'Behold, I will raise up evil against you from your own household; I will even take your wives before your eyes and give them to your companion, and he will lie with your wives in broad daylight. Indeed you did it secretly, but I will do this thing before all Israel, and under the sun'" (1 Sam. 12:11-12). This was later fulfilled during Absalom's rebellion when he publicly violated David's royal concubines as an act of total domination (16:21, 22).

God also raised up the wicked Chaldeans to punish Israel, but then punished the Chaldeans for what they had done to Israel (Hab. 1:6-11). Though God's providence may seem impulsive, vicious, and even unfair to our fallen and finite minds, nevertheless this theme is repeated over and over in the Old Testament. *While God never directly acts wickedly, nor does he take pleasure in evil, he indirectly brings it about through individuals who voluntarily exercise their own wills and are thereby held accountable for their actions.* This is apparent in 2 Samuel 24:1 where we read that "the anger of the LORD burned against Israel, and it incited David against them to say, 'Go, number Israel and Judah.'" Then later, after the census had been taken, David confessed what God had incited him to do was sin (2 Sam. 24:10). It is fascinating to note that even though the LORD incited David to sin (by using Satan to achieve his purposes; see 1 Chron. 21:1), David was clearly held responsible for his actions.

GOD'S SOVEREIGN DECREE FOR CHRIST TO SUFFER

The most striking example of all can be seen in God's providential working in the lives of evil men who, by his sovereign decree, independently chose by their own free will to act wickedly in participating in the crucifixion of the Lord Jesus Christ. None of it caught God by surprise, and neither were their choices a violation of his sovereign will. This was evident in the prayer of Peter and John when they stated, "For truly in this city there were gathered together against Your holy servant Jesus, whom You anointed, both Herod and Pontius Pilate, along with the Gentiles and the peoples of Israel, *to do whatever Your hand and Your purpose predestined to occur*" (Acts 4:27, emphasis added).

Every Christian would do well to remember that the Father's wrath of judgment against sin was poured out upon his Son and our substitute, Jesus Christ. Notwithstanding the responsibility of wicked men who cried out for Jesus to be crucified, Peter made it clear that God ordained his murder when he said, "this Man, delivered up by the *predetermined plan* and *foreknowledge of God*, you nailed to a cross by the hands of godless men and put Him to death" (Acts 2:23, emphasis added).

What an amazing concept: *Jesus willingly chose to suffer and die on a cross because God ordained him to do so.* He was delivered up by the "predetermined plan." The word *predetermined* is the Greek word *horizo,* meaning "to mark out a boundary beforehand," from which we get our English word horizon. The word *plan* translates the Greek word *boule* used in Scripture to describe God's will of purpose; that which he has designed, ordained, or decreed in eternity past. Sometimes this is referred to as his decretive or sovereign will. So Peter is literally saying that *our sovereign God decreed that Jesus die on the cross; it was his predetermined plan.*

Furthermore, he attributes his sacrificial death to the "foreknowledge of God." The word *foreknowledge* is the Greek word *prognosis* meaning "to foreordain"—a meaning that far exceeds the English concept of merely knowing something ahead of time. Moreover, grammatically speaking, since the term is in the instrumental dative case, it must be understood that Peter was actually saying "it was God's foreknowledge (foreordination) that was *the sole cause or the means by which* the men nailed him to a cross."

Said simply, *Jesus did exactly what God ordained him to do, yet those who called for his death and hung him on the tree were responsible for his murder.* Here again we see not only the mysterious convergence and compatibility of God's sovereignty and man's responsibility, but also God deliberately ordaining evil to exist as a part of his plan and purpose to glorify himself—the greatest act of evil in all of history: the murder of Jesus Christ.

Over and over again in Scripture we see a sovereign God orchestrating his universe through the use of both good and evil, a concept perfectly summarized by one of John Calvin's chapter headings in his classic work, *Institutes of the Christian Religion* which states: *God So Uses the Works of the Ungodly, and So Bends Their Minds to Carry Out His Judgments, That He Remains Pure From Every Stain.*[9]

However, we must also understand that God's goodness and justice remain untarnished in all that he does. Moses said, "The Rock! His work is perfect, for all His ways are just; a God of faithfulness and without injustice, righteous and upright is He" (Deut. 32:4). He is the thrice-holy God praised by the seraphim (Isa. 6:3)—holiness being the all-encompassing attribute of God that portrays his hidden glory, his infinite otherness, his incomprehensible transcendence, his consummate perfection, and moral purity. For this reason the apostle John says, "God is Light, and in Him there is no darkness at all" (1 John 1:5).

Despite the inevitable sorrow and suffering of life, we are comforted, knowing, "The Lord's lovingkindnesses indeed never cease, for His compassions never fail. *They* are new every morning; Great is Your faithfulness" (Lam. 3:22-23).

THE SUFFERINGS OF THE APOSTLE PAUL

The apostle Paul's life and ministry as a pioneer church planter provide a remarkable example of the high cost of discipleship Jesus described when he said, "A disciple is not above his teacher, nor a slave above his master" (Matt. 10:24). He understood that he existed to serve Christ. He knew he had been called by God to take the gospel to the Gentiles (Acts 22:21) and he was committed to that end, even if it cost him his life. For this reason he was able to say with calm conviction, "For me, to live is Christ, and to die is gain" (Phil. 1:21). Consider the general summation of his sufferings for the gospel recorded in 2 Corinthians 11:23-33.

Despite all this, Paul remained steadfast in devotion to Christ and content with his suffering. While in a Roman prison he told the saints at Philippi, "I have learned to be content in whatever circumstances I am. I know how to get along with humble means, and I also know how to live in prosperity; in any and every circumstance I have learned the secret of being filled and going hungry, both of having abundance and suffering need. I can do all things through Him who strengthens me" (Phil. 4:11-13).

While in that same prison where he also penned Ephesians, Colossians, and Philemon, the Holy Spirit inspired him to reveal some very important truths that can help us become content with our suffering. I offer three for your consideration.

1. Suffering is a gracious gift from God to help us know Him and experience His felt presence and power in our life.

Few people understand that the inevitable difficulties associated with ministry are ultimately an expression of God's grace in our life; that God is always up to something special in us and through us; and that others are watching and learning.

For this reason Paul writes, "For to you it has been *granted* for Christ's sake, not only to believe in Him, but also to suffer for His sake" (Phil. 1:29-30, emphasis mine). The Greek verb translated *granted* is from the noun for *grace*. Paul is saying that God grants suffering as a gracious favor. When we understand that suffering is a grace gift "for Christ's sake," i.e., in his place, it suddenly takes on a whole new dimension. It is welcomed rather than abhorred. It is the inevitable consequence of "believ[ing] in Him" and the divine path to truly knowing the living God—a concept most professing Christians fail to grasp.

This was Paul's perspective and greatest desire. We see this in his celebrated testimony where he says:

> *I count all things to be loss in view of the*
> *surpassing value of knowing Christ Jesus my Lord,*
> *for whom I have suffered the loss of all things,*
> *and count them but rubbish so that I may gain*
> *Christ, and may be found in Him, not having a*

righteousness of my own derived from the Law,
but that which is through faith in Christ, the
righteousness which comes from God on the basis
of faith, that I may know Him and the power of His
resurrection and the fellowship of His sufferings,
being conformed to His death; in order that I may
attain to the resurrection from the dead.

(Phil. 3:8-11)

When these same convictions are a genuine expression of our heart, we will rejoice in every crucible of grace, knowing it "has been *granted* for Christ's sake" that we might get a glimpse of his glory from yet another angle and persevere in celebratory love and faith in the One who suffered on our behalf and in whose glory we will one day share.

2. Suffering is a grace-granted privilege so that, in our dying, the church may receive life.

Paul expresses this heart attitude in his letter to the Colossians while languishing in a Roman prison when he says, "Now I rejoice in my sufferings for your sake, and in my flesh I do my share *on behalf of His body, which is the church,* in filling up what is lacking in Christ's afflictions" (Col. 1:24, emphasis mine). Paul never allowed his circumstances to rob him of his joy, because he knew that God ordained his afflictions to demonstrate to the church the power of Christ to sustain him and through him continue to build his church. This would have been an amazing testimony to the early saints. Nothing else could explain how a man could press on with such joy and vitality! Paul's suffering had two effects. By it people were either emboldened for the gospel (Phil. 1:14), or in a cowardly way they turned away from it to embrace a gospel more in keeping with the spirit of the age (2 Tim. 1:15; 4:9; 4:16).

By enduring the persecution intended for Christ, he was "filling up what is lacking in Christ's affliction." He was the lightning rod for the world's unending hatred of Christ—a hatred that could not be fully meted out at the cross, but will continue throughout eternity in the blasphemies of the damned (Rev. 16:9-10). Like Christ, Paul was happy to endure an extra measure of suffering as a willing substitute on behalf of the church, perhaps even sparing them untold heartaches while at the same time putting the glory and power of Christ on display.

The kind of hostility he experienced from the deceitful false apostles (2 Cor. 11:13) who gained influence in the Corinthian church was especially brutal. In order to undermine his teaching they had to destroy him personally—a tactic the enemy will use against every faithful servant of Christ. If you can't get him to corrupt the message, then discredit him as the messenger. They accused him of being ugly and unskilled as an orator (he had a low entertainment value), "For they say, 'His letters are weighty and strong, but his bodily presence is weak, and his speech of no account'" (2 Cor. 10:10; cf. 11:6). Because of the brutal torture he endured, his body may have been disfigured (Gal. 6:17). They criticized him for being unloving (2 Cor. 11:7-11) and also made slanderous accusations against his moral integrity, painting him as a deceiver who was cleverly distorting the Old Testament Scripture and twisting the words of Jesus to fit his agenda, to which he responded:

> . . . we do not lose heart, but though our outer man is decaying, yet our inner man is being renewed day by day. For momentary, light affliction is producing for us an eternal weight of glory far beyond all comparison, while we look not at the things which are seen, but at the things which are not seen; for the things which are seen are temporal, but the things which are not seen are eternal.
>
> (2 Cor. 4:1-18)

When we as pastors embrace our afflictions with this perspective, we are able to transcend the pain of our circumstances and persevere with enduring faith, knowing his eternal purposes are being carried out in and through us. Then when the trial has passed—and often in the midst of it—our soul can give testimony of the soul-satisfying joy of being in communion with the living God as he proves himself powerful on our behalf. James summarized it this way:

> Consider it all joy, my brethren, when you encounter various trials, knowing that the

testing of your faith produces endurance. And let
endurance have its perfect result, so that you may
be perfect and complete, lacking in nothing. But
if any of you lacks wisdom, let him ask of God,
who gives to all generously and without reproach,
and it will be given to him.... Blessed is a man
who perseveres under trial; for once he has been
approved, he will receive the crown of life which
the Lord has promised to those who love Him.

(James 1:2-5, 12)

The emphasis is on "those who love Him" and therefore express that love by persevering under trial and obeying (as much as our fallen nature will allow), modeling, teaching, and preaching his commandments, not watering them down to accommodate a culture that is hostile to them.

3. SUFFERING FOR CHRIST, WHEN WILLINGLY EMBRACED, IS A MEANS TO EXPERIENCE DIVINE COMFORT WHEREWITH WE CAN COMFORT OTHERS.

Paul emphasizes this magnificent truth when he says, "For just as the sufferings of Christ are ours in abundance, so also our comfort is abundant through Christ. But if we are afflicted, it is for your comfort and salvation; or if we are comforted, it is for your comfort, which is effective in the patient enduring of the same sufferings which we also suffer; and our hope for you is firmly grounded, knowing that as you are sharers of our sufferings, so also you are sharers of our comfort" (2 Cor. 1:5-7). As an apostle, Paul confronted the same evil forces that caused Christ to suffer even to the point of death. Therefore, everyone who preaches Christ crucified will experience varying measures of that same suffering and thus enjoy the comforting reality of not only being united to Christ in such a convincing way, but also enjoy his reassuring love.

This is one of the deficiencies in some pastors, especially younger ones; they have little experience when it comes to enduring afflictions for the testimony of Christ, and therefore the promised comforts of God are foreign to them and they have little comfort to offer those who suffer greatly. For too many, their faith is all theoretical, not experiential. This is why Paul declared that he, Silvanus, and Timothy "had been approved by God to be entrusted with the gospel" (1 Thess. 2:4). The word "approved" (*dokimadzo*) describes a test to prove whether something is genuine or legitimate. Before Paul was entrusted with the gospel, God tested his faithfulness to it and he was approved. Too many men go into ministry having never been tested or approved.

In time, however, God graciously brings opportunities for us to "stand firm against the schemes of the devil" (Eph. 6:11)—schemes designed to wear us down with adversity, disappointment, and fear, and that cause us to compromise our life and message. This is why we must watch over our heart with all diligence, be aware of the devil's schemes, and be continuously clothed with the full armor of God to be able to stand firm against his schemes. For this reason Paul went on to warn, "Be on the alert with all perseverance and petition for all the saints, and pray on my behalf, that utterance may be given to me in the opening of my mouth, to make known with boldness the mystery of the gospel, for which I am an ambassador in chains; that in proclaiming it I may speak boldly, as I ought to speak" (Eph. 6:18-20).

A Final Word of Exhortation and Encouragement

The ancient priests of Israel had to be men who understood what it meant to "deal gently with the ignorant and the misguided" (Heb. 5:2a). And what was their greatest teacher? The later part of the text gives the answer: ".... since he himself also is beset with weakness" (v. 2b). As pastors, we must be brutally honest and acknowledge our weaknesses. Unless we do, our ministry to others will never be effective. And nothing will expose our weaknesses and give us an opportunity to experience the all-sufficient grace, power, and fellowship of Christ like suffering for him. Knowing this, Paul rejoiced saying, "God's grace is sufficient ... and His power is perfected in weakness.... Most gladly, therefore, I will rather boast about my weaknesses, that the power of Christ may dwell in me" (see 2 Corinthians 12).

Every seasoned shepherd will agree that power in ministry is directly proportional to suffering; the greater our sorrow, the deeper our sympathy; the greater our suffering, the richer our compassion; the greater our willingness to acknowledge our own weaknesses, the greater our dependency on Christ who strengthens us. The inexperienced man fresh out of seminary, the novice counselor fresh out of training, the neophyte evangelist fresh on the mission field—each of these will be of little use until, by God's grace, he has been brought to the end of himself.

As pastors, every time we suffer we are confronted with a profound awareness of our own inadequacies and confronted with the need to depend upon our faithful and sympathetic High Priest to help us "find grace to help in our time of need" (Heb. 4:16). But how can we have a helpless dependence unless we are first made helpless? How can we have true humility unless we are first humbled? How can we deny self and take up our cross daily if we do not have daily crosses and causes to deny self? How can we feel that apart from Christ we can do nothing unless we are made to know by painful experiences that, apart from him, we can do nothing? How can we learn to walk by faith, to embrace a truth and take up a practice solely on the authority and strength of God's Word and not by sight, unless God first removes all the flimsy reeds we try to lean on?

And it is here that we find contentment even in the sorrow and pain. Our trust in God and passion for his glory cannot be manufactured. There is no app for the Christian life. It must be cultivated in the individual who is habitually conversant with him, saturated with his Word, and Spirit-filled. Only then will he embrace suffering *as a gracious gift from God to help him know him and experience his felt presence and power in his life, a grace-granted privilege so that in his dying the church may receive life, and a means to experience divine comfort wherewith he can comfort others.*

To be content with our suffering is certain evidence that the Holy Spirit is active in our life: "If you are reviled for the name of Christ, you are blessed, because the Spirit of glory and of God rests upon you" (1 Peter 4:14). And it is his sanctifying work within us that animates our heart to say with Paul, "I have learned to be content in whatever circumstances I am" (Phil. 4:11).

Like Paul, we must be *consumed with God's glory*, the first and foremost principle for effective ministry. Only then can we be *content with our suffering*, which will make us all the more *convinced of our calling*, the third key principle we will examine in the next chapter.

It Is Well with My Soul

When peace like a river attendeth my way,
When sorrows like sea billows roll;
Whatever my lot, Thou hast taught me to say,
"It is well, it is well with my soul."

Refrain:
It is well with my soul,
It is well with my soul,
It is well, it is well with my soul.

Tho' Satan should buffet, tho' trials should come,
Let this blest assurance control,
That Christ hath regarded my helpless estate,
And hath shed his own blood for my soul.

My sin—O the bliss of this glorious tho't—
My sin—not in part but the whole,
Is nailed to the cross, and I bear it no more,
Praise the Lord, praise the Lord, O my soul!

And, Lord, haste the day when the faith shall be sight,
The clouds be rolled back as a scroll,
The trump shall resound and the Lord shall descend,
"Even so"—it is well with my soul.

Horatio G. Spafford (1828–1888)

CHAPTER 3

KEY PRINCIPLE THREE:
CONVINCED OF HIS CALLING

"Of this church I was made a minister according to the stewardship from God bestowed on me for your benefit, so that I might fully carry out the preaching of the word of God."

Colossians 1:25

During times of great adversity, it is common for a pastor to question his *calling*. He will ask of himself questions like, "Did God really call me to pastoral ministry, or did I just make this whole thing up? If God did call me, why would he allow things to go so terribly wrong? How can I know for sure that God has called me? Or can I?"

What do you tell a man in such distress? What do you say to his dear wife, who will often be equally distraught and disillusioned? Some of the answers have already been addressed in the previous chapter on suffering. But we must also address matters pertaining to a man's call to pastoral ministry. I have discovered that one of the most important convictions necessary to sustain a pastor during the inevitable difficulties of ministry is an unshakeable conviction that he is doing what God has specifically called and gifted him to do. Without such assurance, doubt and discouragement will be his ruin, and Satan will do all in his power to encourage this doubt and deepen the discouragement.

So how does a man know God has *called* him? Does God directly "call a man to preach" as many claim? If so, what constitutes such a call? If not, how can a man know with any degree of certainty that he is serving in a manner God has specifically ordained? These are the concerns that will be addressed in this chapter.

Given his Damascus road encounter and private instruction in the wilderness by Christ himself (Gal. 1:11-17), the apostle Paul was absolutely *convinced of his calling*. He stated, "Of this church I was made a minister according to the stewardship from God bestowed on me for your benefit, so that I might fully carry out the preaching of the word of God" (Col. 1:25). Even when his own calling was vigorously attacked and he was accused of being a false apostle, his conviction never waned. There were times when he thought he had run in vain, but not that he had been mistaken in running.

By his own testimony we see the level of boldness that resulted from his confidence in having been called by God:

> . . . *we have been approved by God to be entrusted with the gospel, so we speak, not as pleasing men, but God who examines our hearts. For we never*

> *came with flattering speech, as you know, nor*
> *with a pretext for greed—God is witness.*
>
> *(1 Thess. 2:4-5)*

Paul knew beyond a shadow of a doubt that he had been divinely called to be "the steward of God" (Titus 1:7); a calling that evoked within him a level of humility so powerful that he wanted others to see him and his fellow ministers as "fellow workers" (1 Cor. 3:9), "servants of Christ and stewards of the mysteries of God" (4:1). Every potential pastor must share this humble conviction. Without it, his pride will cause him to falter and fail.

Discerning a Man's Calling and Church Leadership

With Paul as an example, it is clear that this matter of a divine call to vocational ministry is important for every church leader to understand and embrace. One of the most destructive decisions a church can make is to put a man in leadership who has not been tested and approved, which requires far more than a seminary degree as we will see. My mind is flooded with horror stories of churches that have allowed self-appointed, unqualified pastors and elders to lead them, some for generations. Many so-called "pastors" today are nothing more than entrepreneurs peddling the gospel, wolves fleecing the sheep. Churches led by such men (and women in some instances) will fill up with goats that will eventually overpower the sheep, tares that will choke out the wheat, nonbelievers who will consider the things of the Spirit to be foolishness (1 Cor. 2:14).

In his book *Lectures to My Students*, the great nineteenth-century English preacher, Charles Haddon Spurgeon, offered compelling insights concerning the great danger of placing a man into vocational ministry who thinks he has been called to that position when in fact he has not. Spurgeon asks,

> *How may a young man know whether he is called or not? That is a weighty inquiry, and I desire to treat it most solemnly. Oh, for divine guidance in so doing! That*

hundreds have missed their way and stumbled against a pulpit is sorrowfully evident from the fruitless ministries and decaying churches which surround us. It is a fearful calamity to a man to miss his calling, and to the church upon whom he imposes himself, his mistake involves an affliction of the most grievous kind. It would be a curious and painful subject for reflection—the frequency with which men in the possession of reason mistake the end of their existence, and aim at objects which they were never intended to pursue.[10]

What a refreshing contrast we see in the apostle Paul, who was absolutely certain his calling was from God. This was validated by the undeniable power of his life and message—not to mention the spiritual fruit he manifested that could only be attributed to a branch abiding in the "true vine" which is Christ himself (John 15:5). Without this conviction, pastors will operate in the flesh, not the Spirit, and gradually wither away in a fruitless ministry. Time and time again in those seasons of great sorrow and adversity as a pastor, it has been the absolute certainty of my calling that has emboldened and empowered me to get up off my face, pick up my sword, and get back into the battle.

Another nineteenth-century English preacher and theologian, Charles Bridges, underscored the profound importance of a man knowing for sure that God has called him to undertake such a daunting task:

To labour in the dark, without an assured commission, greatly obscures the warrant of faith in the Divine engagements; and the Minister, unable to avail himself of heavenly support, feels his "hands hang down, and his knees feeble" in his work. On the other hand, the confidence that he is acting in obedience to the call of God—that he is in his work, and in his way—nerves him in the midst of all difficulty, and under a sense of his responsible obligations, with almighty strength.[11]

Every man who claims to serve Christ in this way must be able to say with Paul: "I have been approved by God to be entrusted with the gospel" (1 Thess. 2:4). Armed with such Spirit-empowered confidence, he will be ready for the fight.

TESTS OF DIVINE CALLING TO VOCATIONAL MINISTRY

But how can a man have confidence that God has specifically called him to be a pastor? Asked differently, what are the tests of such a divine calling, if any? I would humbly suggest five categories that emerge from Scripture and can be affirmed by the personal experience of every faithful pastor. He must have the following:

1. A longing to know and serve Christ;

2. A sense of urgency to preach the gospel;

3. A pervasive feeling of inadequacy;

4. A burden to shepherd the flock;

5. A public confirmation of spiritual gifts, character, and abilities.

I invite you to join me in examining these categories more closely.

TEST NUMBER ONE:
A LONGING TO KNOW AND SERVE CHRIST

Martyn Lloyd-Jones once said, "If a person does not love fundamental truths, and desire to know them more, he has no claim to be regarded as a Christian."[12] Any man who has no longing to know more of Christ and give his life in service to him is certainly not fit to be his chosen overseer, and has not been called to do so. For many men, that desire is there, but it is too weak to endure the journey of pastoral ministry. The proper attitude commended for such a calling is stated in Paul's introduction to the necessary qualifications of the office. He says, "If any man aspires to the office of overseer, it is a fine work he desires to do." The verb translated "aspires" (*oregomai*) means literally "to stretch oneself" or "reach out one's hand." Figuratively it means, "to aspire, to strive for, or desire something."[13] Perhaps the most vivid illustration is that of a runner straining every fiber of muscle in his body to stretch himself out as he approaches the finish line.

The second verb, translated "desires" (*epithumeo*), means "to long for" and is comparable to the expression "set one's heart on."[14] So Paul is saying that any man who is stretching out with all his being to serve Christ as one of his under-shepherds is doing so because he has an inner longing to labor in that capacity. This kind of aspiration finds its source in the Spirit's work in a man's heart, a supernatural calling and gifting fueled by a man's longing to know and serve Christ. Clearly it is not the *office* he seeks, but the *service*; an opportunity to labor for the Master he lovingly adores and seeks to know more fully. If the desire is sincere, God accepts the desire for the deed and blesses according to faithfulness. This is a great encouragement for those whose labor seems to be spent in vain in what appears to be a fruitless ministry.

What hypocrisy for a man to claim to be an under-shepherd of the Great Shepherd when he has no yearning to experience more of his infinite glory, greatness, and power. What man can possibly speak accurately of the unsearchable riches of Christ when he himself has no private devotion to him or intimate fellowship with him? What branch can possibly bear the fruit of Christlikeness if it has little desire to abide in the Vine of Christ himself as he has commanded? Has he not said, "for apart from Me you can do nothing" (John 15:5)? How can a man pray in harmony with the will of God if the Lord is a stranger to him and God's Word is not flowing through his veins? No man can ever be saturated with the Word of Christ apart from a passionate longing to continually abide in his presence; only then can he "ask whatever [he] wish, and it will be done for [him]" (v. 7).

Only when a man has an insatiable desire to know more of Christ will he experience the soul-satisfying joy of his presence deep within his soul, and only then will he be a fit vessel for the Master's use. If this is missing in a man considering pastoral ministry, he has failed the first and most important test, and should first do a thorough and brutally honest examination of his heart to see if he is indeed a Christian.

We would do well to learn from the Puritans in this regard. Richard Baxter, the noble seventeenth-century Puritan pastor at Kidderminster, England, summarized this issue with great insight and conviction:

Alas! It is the common danger and calamity of the Church, to have unregenerate and inexperienced pastors, and to have so many men become preachers before they are Christians; who are sanctified by dedication to the altar as the priests of God, before they are sanctified by hearty dedication as the disciples of Christ; and so to worship an unknown God, and to preach an unknown Christ, to pray through an unknown Spirit, to recommend a state of holiness and communion with God, and a glory and a happiness which are all unknown, and like to be unknown to them for ever. He is like to be but a heartless preacher, that hath not the Christ and grace that he preacheth, in his heart. O that all our students in our universities would well consider this! What a poor business is it to themselves, to spend their time in acquiring some little knowledge of the works of God, and of some of those names which the divided tongues of the nations have imposed on them, and not to know God himself, nor exalt him in their hearts, nor to be acquainted with that one renewing work that should make them happy! They do but "walk in a vain show," and spend their lives like dreaming men, while they busy their wits and tongues about abundance of names and notions, and are strangers to God and the life of saints. If ever God awaken them by his saving grace, they will have cogitations and employments so much more serious than their unsanctified studies and disputations, that they will confess they did but dream before. A world of business they make themselves about nothing, while they are willful strangers to the primitive, independent, necessary Being, who is all in all. Nothing can be rightly known, if God be not known; nor is any study well managed, nor to any great purpose, if God is not studied. We know little of the creature, till we know it as it stands related to the Creator.[15]

Once again, a man may be quite certain he is truly regenerate, yet still have no *longing to know and experience Christ*. If this is the case, he is mistaken and self-deceived and has never been made a new creature in Christ. Those who have truly tasted the kindness of God will long for the pure milk of the Word. If there is no spiritual hunger, there is no spiritual life.

But there are men who truly know Christ, yet find themselves so distracted with the affairs of life, and perhaps weighted down with besetting sins, that their desire to know and experience him has been greatly diminished. Paul warned Timothy of this danger when he said, "No soldier in active service entangles himself in the affairs of everyday life, so that he may please the one who enlisted him as a soldier" (2 Tim. 2:4). If, after a solemn inquiry of the soul this proves to be the case, such a man must not continue on a path of vocational ministry. He is neither qualified nor outfitted for such a journey and will eventually collapse in exhaustion on the way.

The Old Testament saints spoke often of an inward enjoyment of God that motivated their worshipful praise, adoration, and service to God in heart and life. We see this in David's reference to "God my exceeding joy" (Ps. 43:4), and also when the psalmist declares with great passion, "O taste and see that the Lord is good; how blessed is the man who takes refuge in Him!" (Ps. 34:8). A man considering pastoral ministry must ask:

○ "Do I think often of the love of Christ and his electing grace in my life?"

○ "Does his goodness toward me flood my soul with joy inexpressible and animate my heart to look to him for more?"

○ "Does his love for me evoke such a solemn sense of debt I owe as to motivate me to give my very life for him?"

Unless a minister has this kind of breathless adoration for Christ, he has no business being his ambassador, nor has God called him to be one.

The apostle Paul's longing for an ever-increasing level of intimate fellowship with Christ leaps off every page he wrote. We see this, for example, in his poignant words to the Philippians: "I count all things to be loss in view of the surpassing value of knowing Christ Jesus my Lord, for whom I have suffered the loss of all things, and count them but rubbish so that I may gain Christ" (Phil. 3:8).

The great tragedy among many young men entering the ministry is that they are more excited about the *office* than about *Christ*. They have little enjoyment of "the love of God" that "has been poured out within our hearts through the Holy Spirit who was given to us" (Rom. 5:5). Countless ministers have gradually withered away into fruitlessness because of this. The devil convinces them they are right with God—validated by all the religious activities they do and the applause they receive. But in reality they have failed to cultivate the garden of their soul through intimate fellowship with Christ. It is simply not a priority of their heart.

In his moving book, *The Thought of God*, Scottish pastor Maurice Roberts offered the following insights regarding this matter of knowing and experiencing "Christ, the Lover of Our Souls":

> *Ecstasy and delight are essential to the believer's soul and they promote sanctification. We were not meant to live without spiritual exhilaration and the Christian who goes for a long time without the experience of heart-warming will soon find himself tempted to have his emotions satisfied from earthly things and not, as he ought, from the Spirit of God. The soul is so constituted that it craves fulfillment from things outside itself and will embrace earthly joys for satisfaction when it cannot reach spiritual ones. Not for nothing did Satan draw Eve to see that the forbidden fruit grew on a tree which was "pleasant to the eyes" and on a "tree to be desired." The believer is in spiritual danger if he allows himself to go for any length of time without tasting the love of Christ and savouring the felt comforts of a Saviour's presence. When Christ ceases to fill the heart with satisfaction, our souls will go in silent search of other lovers.*[16]

The apostle Paul understood and experienced the soul-exhilarating joy of a *felt Christ*. This is what drove him to faithful service and obedience. He knew firsthand what it was like to enjoy the divine presence of Christ. For this reason he could say, "For me to live is Christ and to die is gain" (Phil. 1:21).

Every man considering vocational ministry must be brutally honest and ask himself, "Can I say with David: 'As the deer pants for the water brooks, so my soul pants for You, O God. My soul thirsts for God, for the living God' (Ps. 42:1-2a)?" If the answer is *no*, he has no sense of his inward poverty for what only the Lord can provide. He therefore leaves himself vulnerable to personal sin and ministry failure.

I've counseled many broken and burned-out pastors who had to admit that although they had remained orthodox in doctrine and practice, their love for Christ had grown cold. They were like the church in Ephesus of whom the Lord said, "But I have this against you, that you have left your first love" (Rev. 2:4). The only thing worse than a pastor forsaking his fervent love for Christ, albeit unwittingly, is for a man to have entered the ministry without ever having it. Such a man may be a walking library of biblical knowledge, a veritable treasure trove of theological acumen, and a Spurgeon in the pulpit, but if he has no yearning for Christ in secret godliness, *he is nothing.* Perhaps John Owen said it best, "What [a] minister is on his knees in secret before God Almighty, that he is and no more."[7]

In light of these considerations, I would challenge all men contemplating vocational ministry to examine their heart and ask, "Do I have a longing to know and experience Christ?" If you fail this test, you have no business serving Christ as his choice servant, nor have you been called to do so.

TEST NUMBER TWO:
A SENSE OF URGENCY TO PREACH THE GOSPEL

Ask any faithful pastor whose ministry has obviously been blessed by God and he will tell you that one of the primary reasons he was certain God had called him to be a pastor was his unrelenting sense of urgency to preach the gospel—which includes the whole counsel of God revealed in Scripture. He will acknowledge how his innermost being panted after the things of God, and his desire to minister was so strong that all the riches and power in the world were utterly meaningless to him in comparison.

God's call to pastoral ministry will never be a sudden urge out of nowhere; rather, *it will be an unshakeable longing of the soul, a solemn apprehension of the inner man that will not let him go.* After solemn inquiry during long seasons of prayer for clarity, a man will have an inescapable sense of urgency that mixes joy with fear, zeal with apprehension, and duty with desire.

Spurgeon put it this way:

We must feel that woe is unto us if we preach not the gospel; the Word of God must be unto us as fire in our bones, otherwise, if we undertake the ministry, we shall be unhappy in it, shall be unable to bear the self-denials incident to it, and shall be of little service to those among whom we minister. I speak of self-denials, and well I may; for the true pastor's work is full of them, and without a love to his calling, he will soon succumb, and either leave the drudgery or move on in discontent, burdened with a monotony as tiresome as that of a blind horse in a mill. . . . Girded with that love, you will be undaunted; divested of that more-than-magic belt of irresistible vocation, you will pine away in wretchedness. [18]

Obviously, having *a sense of urgency to preach the gospel* is something far different than having a desire to stand in front of an audience to be the center of attention and receive accolades of praise. The man whom God has called will have a heavy burden for the salvation and sanctification of men's souls for the glory of Christ. A man considering pastoral ministry must ask himself this: "Do I have a longing to see them *come to know, love, worship, and serve Christ?*" Evangelism and discipleship must be the overwhelming, all-absorbing craving within his soul, otherwise the inevitable sorrows of ministry will soon drive him to despair.

A true minister of the gospel must be so burdened for the lost that he will say with Paul, "I have great sorrow and unceasing grief in my heart. For I could wish that I myself were accursed, separated from Christ for the sake of my brethren, my kinsmen according to the flesh" (Rom. 9:2-3) . . . "my heart's desire and prayer to God for them is that they may be saved" (10:1). This priority dominated Paul's ministry. For this reason he reminded the Corinthians, "For I determined to know nothing among you except Jesus Christ, and Him crucified" (1 Cor. 2:2).

Every sincere pastor will be like Jeremiah, who, despite enormous resistance and threats to his life, could not stop preaching because, "there is in my heart as it were a burning fire shut up in my bones, and I am weary with holding it in and I cannot" (Jer. 20:9). And Jeremiah preached for more than forty years, over half of which was during the unparalleled religious reforms of Josiah, yet without a single convert. In fact, he was told (as was Ezekiel) at the beginning of his ministry that no one would listen to him, but to preach anyway. In our day, many can expect to be in a Jeremiah-type ministry. This requires the conviction of a sincere call and the shared burden of Paul who said, "Woe to me if I do not preach the gospel" (1 Cor. 9:16). This is what it means to have *a sense of urgency to preach the gospel!*

If a man considering pastoral ministry cannot honestly identify with such a passionate burden to unleash the only truth that can make sinners right with God and avoid his judgment in eternal hell, he has no legitimate reason to stand behind a pulpit to preach. He must admit what others will soon detect: *God simply has not called him to pastoral ministry.*

TEST NUMBER THREE:
A PERVASIVE FEELING OF INADEQUACY

This third test is perfectly summarized in Paul's reflection upon the daunting task of gospel ministry and his own deficiencies when he said, "Who is adequate for these things?" (2 Cor. 2:16). Obviously, he knew his strength and competence were insufficient. When Paul came to Corinth to first preach the gospel to that exceedingly wicked city, notorious for its moral degeneracy and idolatry, he reminded the saints that he did so "in weakness and in fear and in much trembling, and my message and my preaching were not in persuasive words of wisdom, but in demonstration of the Spirit and of power, so that your faith would not rest on the wisdom of men, but on the power of God" (1 Cor. 2:3-5).

Paul was fully aware of his inadequacy and utter dependence upon the Spirit's power. This does not mean he was a wilting lily, afraid to preach. He was utterly fearless in his preaching! But he was humble enough to be suspect of his own spirituality— so much so that he asked the saints at Ephesus to "pray on my behalf ... that I may speak boldly, as I ought to speak" (Eph. 6:19-20).

Paul's "weakness" (1 Cor. 2:3) is a reference to the *perceived weakness* of the simple, unadorned gospel message considered to be a stumbling block to the Jews and foolishness to the Gentiles. He knew there was a high probability his message would be rejected. He also knew there was nothing he could say or do to cause anyone to believe. Yet, as he stated in verses 25 and 27, the *perceived weakness of the gospel* was actually the power of God to deliver sinners from the power and penalty of sin, and for good reason: "Because the foolishness of God is wiser than men, and the weakness of God is stronger than men . . . but God has chosen the foolish things of the world to shame the wise, and God has chosen the weak things of the world to shame the things which are strong."

His reference to coming to them in "fear and in much trembling" is a phrase he used in other passages in the context of being deeply burdened over a specific matter.[19] And with the Corinthians, as well as all the other places he preached, he was indeed *afraid* that people would reject the message of the cross and he *trembled* over the eternal consequences of hell that would be their fate. By contrast, none of this characterized the hearts of the Greek philosophers the Corinthians were so enamored with; and I fear it is equally foreign to many men in pulpits today who secretly see themselves as being adequate to the task. Charles Spurgeon offers additional insight into this solemn truth:

> *The power that is in the Gospel does not lie in the eloquence of the preacher, otherwise men would be the converters of souls, nor does it lie in the preacher's learning, otherwise it would consist in the wisdom of men. We might preach until our tongues rotted, till we would exhaust our lungs and die, but never a soul would be converted unless the Holy Spirit be with the Word of God to give it the power to convert the soul.*[20]

Would that every preacher of the gospel embrace the reality of his inadequacies and utter dependence upon the Spirit to accomplish anything. It is all too easy for a young man considering the ministry to unwittingly overestimate his abilities and think he is able on his own to accomplish God's purposes in God's way. I have seen this many times with untested men fresh out of seminary who assume that their degrees and the decorations of honors on their graduation gowns prove their spiritual prowess and readiness to shepherd. But such is never the case. Refining fires are sure to come.

If ever a man could have been justified in thinking his abilities proved he was up for the task, it would have been Paul. However, despite his supreme qualifications, the Lord made it clear to him that ongoing refinement was still necessary. We see this in the situation of his "thorn in the flesh" (2 Cor. 12:7). After he had pleaded three times to the Lord (prayers directed to Jesus himself) for the relief of this agonizing obstacle to ministry, the Lord revealed to him the purpose of the pain: "a messenger of Satan" was sent "to harass [him], to keep [him] from becoming conceited" (2 Cor. 12:7).[21] With this understanding, Paul humbly rejoiced in God's response to him:

> He has said to me, "My grace is sufficient for you, for power is perfected in weakness." Most gladly, therefore, I will rather boast about my weaknesses, so that the power of Christ may dwell in me. Therefore I am well content with weaknesses, with insults, with distresses, with persecutions, with difficulties, for Christ's sake; for when I am weak, then I am strong.
>
> (2 Cor. 12:9-10)

This demonstrates the divine priority for his servants to be both humble and dependent upon the constant availability of his all-sufficient grace. He understood that "the light of the knowledge of the glory of God in the face of Jesus Christ" was a "treasure in jars of clay, to show that the surpassing power belongs to God and not to us" (2 Cor. 4:6-7).

While every faithful shepherd will experience times when the Lord will ignite fires of adversity in order to temper the steel of his faith, the importance of having *a pervasive feeling of inadequacy* from the outset of vocational ministry must not be underestimated. It is a major test of divine calling. Without it, a man will certainly fail, because, "Pride *goes* before destruction, and a haughty spirit before stumbling" (Prov. 16:18).

TEST NUMBER FOUR:
A BURDEN TO SHEPHERD THE FLOCK

Someone has well said, "A shepherd will smell like sheep." So true! Because of his compassion for those God has entrusted to him, a faithful pastor will spend his life nurturing, feeding, protecting, and leading his flock. He will have a desire to shepherd sheep, not herd goats. While this will take time to develop more fully after a man enters the ministry, *his compassion for others must be evident prior to it.*

I've known men who say they love their congregation, and even get angry if anyone suggests otherwise, but their glowing self-evaluation does not reflect the candid observations of many in the church—especially those outside the sphere of their closest friends and sycophants. Any man considering vocational ministry must have an enthusiastic recommendation from his church family that indeed he is a man known for his sacrificial love and devotion to *everyone* he encounters—like Timothy who "was well spoken of by the brethren who were in Lystra and Iconium" (Acts 16:2). A man who truly loves Christ will truly love *all* those who belong to Christ. Sacrificial, selfless love will define his character. It will be obvious to all who experience him, and he will secretly lament that he loves so little. This supreme virtue will also add weight to his burden to shepherd his flock.

A true under-shepherd will emulate the chief Shepherd, who wept over Jerusalem (Luke 19:41) and "loved the church" so much he "gave Himself up for her" (Eph. 5:25). Because of his sacrificial love for his flock, a true shepherd will feel an ever-present burden for the spiritual welfare of those God has placed under his care. Paul expressed this when he said to the saints in Corinth, "Apart from such external things, there is the daily pressure on me of concern for all the churches" (2 Cor. 11:28) "...I will most gladly spend and be expended for your souls" (12:15).

A man truly called by God will have this kind of reputation among fellow believers before he enters the ministry. He will imitate Paul, who imitated Christ (1 Cor. 11:1); who among the Thessalonians was like a *godly mother*, characterized by tender devotion, deep affection, sacrificial love, and selfless labor; and like a *godly father* he had a heart dedicated to holy living and biblical instruction (1 Thess. 2:7-12).

Perhaps the most explicit yet overlooked books in the New Testament defining the character and responsibilities of a pastor are 1 and 2 Thessalonians. Richard Mayhue's careful analysis of these epistles provides an eye-opening description of what a pastor is to be and what he must do, each underscoring the profound importance of having a burden to shepherd the flock. According to Mayhue, a pastor's main responsibilities include:

1. Praying   (1 Thess. 1:2-5; 3:9-13)

2. Evangelizing   (1 Thess. 1:4-5; 9-10)

3. Equipping   (1 Thess. 1:6-8)

4. Defending   (1 Thess. 2:1-6)

5. Loving   (1 Thess. 2:7-8)

6. Laboring   (1 Thess. 2:9)

7. Modeling   (1 Thess. 2:10)

8. Leading   (1 Thess. 2:10-12)

9. Feeding   (1 Thess. 2:13)

10. Watching   (1 Thess. 3:1-8)

11. Warning   (1 Thess. 4:1-8)

12. Teaching   (1 Thess. 4:9-5:11)

13. Exhorting   (1 Thess. 5:12-24)

14. Encouraging   (2 Thess. 1:3-12)

15. Correcting   (2 Thess. 2:1-12)

16. Confronting   (2 Thess. 3:6, 14)

17. Rescuing   (2 Thess. 3:15)[22]

Without a genuine burden to shepherd the saints, no man can be devoted to these responsibilities. No man can emulate Paul by "serving the Lord with all humility and with tears and with trials" (Acts 20:19), as a faithful messenger who "did not shrink from declaring . . . anything that was profitable, and teaching . . . in public and from house to house" (v. 20).

There is no place in the church for lazy pastors who are indifferent to the spiritual needs of their flock, or entrepreneurial pastors who are motivated by money, or power-hungry pastors who *drive* their sheep rather than *lead* them. Instead, he must be such an example of compassionate care that others not only experience it, but are also moved to *imitate* it. With these concerns in mind Peter exhorts elders to:

> *Shepherd the flock of God among you, exercising*
> *oversight not under compulsion, but voluntarily,*
> *according to the will of God; and not for sordid*
> *gain, but with eagerness; nor yet as lording it*
> *over those allotted to your charge, but proving to*
> *be examples to the flock.*
>
> *(1 Peter 5:2-3)*

Without exception, the men who have had the greatest impact on my life have been those who loved me enough to intentionally come alongside me with words of encouragement and warning. This is what real shepherding looks like. It is the outworking of a man's inner burden to see people come to love and serve Christ. A true shepherd will joyfully give of himself as Christ gave of himself. He will have such a deep concern to protect his flock from error and experience the exhilarating joy of gospel living that he will echo the words of Paul who said, "My children, with whom I am again in labor until Christ is formed in you" (Gal. 4:19).

Unfortunately, this is often a neglected duty. Most members of a congregation have little contact with their shepherd(s) one-on-one. Yet it is in the context of face-to-face intentional interaction that the Word is best brought to bear upon the practical issues of their lives. In this context a pastor can really hear their heart, learn about their objections and doctrinal errors, and, most importantly, garner important insights into their personal struggles and sins.

It is in the framework of private oversight where they can be most effectively established in their faith. This is where the pastor wins their affections, builds their trust, learns what he must pray for and guard against, knowing he will one day give an account regarding his faithfulness in "keeping watch care over [their] souls" (Heb. 13:17).

Once again, the faithful Puritan pastor Richard Baxter addresses this with utmost somberness:

It is too common for men to think that the work of the ministry is nothing but to preach, and to baptize, and to administer the Lord's supper, and to visit the sick. By this means the people will submit to no more; and too many ministers are such strangers to their own calling that they will do no more. It hath oft grieved my heart to observe some eminent able preachers, how little they do for the saving of souls, save only in the pulpit; and to how little purpose much of their labour is, by this neglect. They have hundreds of people that they never spoke a word to personally for their salvation; and if we may judge by their practice, they consider it not as their duty; and the principal thing that hardeneth men in this oversight is the common neglect of the private part of the work by others.

There are so few that do much in it, and the omission hath grown so common among pious, able men, that the disgrace of it is abated by their ability; and a man may now be guilty of it without any particular notice or dishonour. Never doth sin so reign in a church or state, as when it hath gained reputation, or, at least, is no disgrace to the sinner, nor a matter of offence to beholders. But I make no doubt, through the mercy of God, that the restoring of the practice of personal oversight will convince many ministers, that this is as truly their work as that which they now do, and may awaken to see that the ministry is another kind of business than too many excellent preachers take it to be.

Brethren, do but set yourselves closely to this work, and follow it diligently; and though you do it silently, without any words to them that are negligent, I am in hope that most of you who are present may live to see the day when the neglect of private personal oversight of all the flock shall be taken for a scandalous and odious omission.[23]

If a man considering vocational ministry demonstrates no desire to be personally involved in one-on-one discipleship, his perspective of pastoral ministry is greatly flawed and he deceives himself. While this important duty can and must be developed more fully over time, it must be a commitment held in equal esteem as public preaching. If not, God has not called him to shepherd his flock.

Practically speaking, we are to disciple men so they can shepherd their own wives and children. God lays this responsibility on each Christian man, not on the church (Eph. 5:25-33; 6:4; 1 Cor. 14:34-35). It is the men that God will hold accountable, not the church, especially in an age when truth is so easily accessible. Most have abdicated this responsibility to the church. Part of this one-on-one discipleship must be calling people to fulfill their God-ordained responsibilities. If a man considering the pastorate is personally deficient in shepherding his wife and children, he will not make this a priority in his ministry and as a result forfeit blessing in his life and in his church.

Jonathan Edwards addressed this in his diary during the Half-Way Covenant controversy. He first addresses ministers.

A minister by his office is to be the guide and instructor of his people. To that end he is to study and search the Scriptures and to teach the people, not the opinions of men—of other divines or of their ancestors—but the mind of Christ. As he is set to enlighten them, so a part of his duty is to rectify their mistakes, and, if he sees them out of the way of truth or duty, to be a voice behind them, saying, "This is the way, walk ye in it." Hence, if what he offers to exhibit to them as the mind of Christ be different from their previous apprehensions, unless it be on some point which is established in the church of God as fundamental, surely they are obliged to hear him. If not, there is an end at once to all the use and benefit of teachers in the church in these respects—as the means of increasing its light and knowledge, and reclaiming it from mistakes and errors. This would be in effect to establish, not the word of Christ, but the opinion of the last generation in each town and church, as an immutable rule to all future generations to the end of the world.[24]

Edwards then addresses fathers directly, underscoring the kind of one-on-one discipleship in which every father (and pastor) must be engaged.

Particularly inquire whether you do not live in sin, by living in the neglect of instructing them. Do you not wholly neglect the duty of instructing your children, or if you do not wholly neglect it, yet do you not afford them so little instruction, and are you not so unsteady, and do you not take so little pains in it, that you live in sinful neglect? Do you take pains in any measure proportionate to the importance of the matter? Are you as careful about the welfare of their souls as you are their bodies? Do you labor as much that they may have eternal life, as you do to provide estates for them to live on in this world? . . . Do you not live in sinful neglect of the government of your families? Do you not live in the sin of Eli, who indeed counseled and reproved his children, but did not exercise government over them? . . . If you say you cannot restrain your children, this is no excuse; for it is a sign that you have brought up your children without government, that your children regard not your authority. When parents lose their government over their children, their reproofs and counsel signify but little. . . . By neglect in this particular, parents bring the guilt of their children's sins upon their own souls, and the blood of their children will be required at their hands.[25]

TEST NUMBER FIVE:
A PUBLIC CONFIRMATION OF SPIRITUAL GIFTS, CHARACTER, AND ABILITIES

In an ancient world of self-appointed frauds and false apostles, Paul testified to his divine commission by declaring, "We have been approved by God to be entrusted with the gospel" (1 Thess. 2:4). This is a fascinating statement. The perfect tense verb "have been approved" indicates that *some careful evaluation in the past resulted in his present state of approval.* Despite being chosen by God to be an apostle before he was born (Gal. 1:15), even Paul was subject to a time of *testing, training,* and *examination* prior to being entrusted with the gospel. Only then did God set his seal of approval on him for gospel ministry. Far too many men enter seminary, and are accepted by seminaries, who have never even taught a Bible study, much less had their devotion to truth tested by fire.

In fact, Paul himself calls all churches to examine those who are appointed to positions of leadership: "Whoever thus serves Christ is acceptable to God and approved by men" (Rom. 14:18). The requirement for an elder to be tested and affirmed is evident in the qualifications listed in 1 Timothy 3:1-7 and Titus 1:6-9, and even extends with some variation to deacons where Paul says, "Let them also be tested first; then let them serve as deacons if they prove themselves blameless" (1 Tim. 3:10). But clearly with respect to elders he warns, "Do not lay hands upon anyone too hastily and thus share responsibility for the sins of others" (1 Tim. 5:22).

This is a very important warning that all too often goes unheeded. Hasty ordinations almost inevitably turn out to be disastrous. Unqualified men placed into ministry wreak havoc in a church, and those responsible for placing them there are culpable of misleading the people and indirectly condoning that man's sins. Paul went on to warn, "The sins of some men are quite evident, going before them to judgment; for others, their sins follow after" (v. 24). Once again, this underscores the importance of careful scrutiny during the evaluation process. Some men's sins are so obvious a congregation can easily judge them and see they are disqualified. But the sins of others are not so readily apparent.

Early on in ministry, I was guilty of affirming men as elders who I thought were reasonably well-qualified, then later I discovered areas of sin that were unacceptable and divisive. Sadly, most men inherit a less-than-qualified elder board. This often happens in small churches where a pastor has few men to choose from. The tendency is to choose the best you have and hope for the best, even if the men chosen are only moderately qualified. Then, to your dismay, you later discover you've affirmed a control freak, or a contentious hothead, or a Deputy Barney Fife who now has a bullet, a badge, and little black book, and he's putting everyone in jail—a little authority can bring out the worst in some men (see 1 Tim. 3:6). So I have learned the hard way that it is far better to spend more time scrutinizing men on the front end than to go through the painful process of trying to get rid of them on the back end.

Men being considered for full-time vocational ministry need even greater scrutiny. Because we are all hopelessly biased in our own favor, we need the honest evaluation of others who are spiritually discerning in these matters to give us their critique and recommendation. Wise and seasoned pastors will know how a congregation will respond, especially as it relates to preaching and teaching.

We've all watched *American Idol* hopefuls embarrass themselves in front of the world with a vocal performance fit only for the shower. Because they sang solos in school musicals and in church, they were quite certain stardom would be their destiny. Many would-be preachers who are weak communicators are no different. If a man has no natural ability to speak clearly and compellingly, we do him and the body of Christ a grave disservice by praising him just to make him feel good. When it comes to preaching, there's no such thing as a participation award. We have all endured men bereft of the most basic abilities drone on and on while we all fidget to stay awake. There are many ways God can lull men to sleep, but his messengers are not to be one of them.

As in any area of Christian service, a man will hone his homiletical skills and develop other aspects of his giftedness over time. But there must be some basic and noticeable natural abilities to build upon. A man's spiritual gifts, character, and abilities must be obvious to others and he must be evaluated by those qualified to do so. We see this in the case of Timothy. Paul originally chose him as a companion because "he was well spoken of by the brothers at Lystra and Iconium" (Acts 16:2). However, we must be careful to distinguish between natural talents and spiritual gifts. Some men have great natural talents of communication who later prove to be wolves in sheep's clothing.

Ultimately a man must be scrutinized by recognized leaders; then, after much prayer, he can be formally set apart for his office consistent with the New Testament concept of ordination. We see this biblical precedent in Acts 14:23: "When they had appointed elders for them in every church, with prayer and fasting they committed them to the Lord in whom they had believed." The Holy Spirit asked the godly prophets and teachers in the church of Antioch to "set apart for Me Barnabas and Saul for the work to which I have called them." Then after fasting and praying they "laid their hands on them and sent them off" (Acts 13:2-3).

Because Christ purchased his church with his very blood, it is of utmost importance that we be careful in selecting and appointing men to any position of spiritual leadership, especially the office of pastor-teacher. Paul's exhortation to the elders in Ephesus affirms this when he says, "Pay careful attention to yourselves and to all the flock, in which the Holy Spirit has made you overseers, to care for the church of God" (Acts 20:28). If a man does not willingly and joyfully subject himself to this kind of scrutiny, he has no basis to claim God has called him to the pastorate. Moreover, if there is not public confirmation of his spiritual gifts, character, and abilities, he fails the most important test.

Charles Spurgeon's familiar warning had a great impact on my life when I was wrestling with these issues early on in my ministry, and is so fitting in this regard. He warned:

> *Do not enter the ministry if you can help it. . . . If any student in this room could be content to be a newspaper editor, or a grocer, or a farmer, or a doctor, or a lawyer, or a senator, or a king, in the name of heaven and earth let him go his way; he is not the man in whom dwells the Spirit of God in its fullness, for a man so filled with God would utterly weary of any pursuit but that for which his inmost soul pants.*[26]

FINAL WORD

Once again, I would challenge all men contemplating vocational ministry to examine their heart under the light of these five categories. If indeed you can say with sincerity that you have *a longing to know and serve Christ, a sense of urgency to preach the gospel, a pervasive feeling of inadequacy, a burden to shepherd the flock,* your testimony will result in *a public confirmation of spiritual gifts, character, and abilities.*

Given this, God's providence will then lead you to the specific place where he will have you serve him. In light of this you can rejoice in Christ's promise: "I will build My church" (Matt. 16:18). Be encouraged, knowing Christ has pledged to be personally involved in your ministry. You are not alone, as Paul made clear in his statement to the Corinthians, "For we are God's fellow workers" (1 Cor. 3:9).

Amazed and humbled by the highest of all honors God can confer upon any man, you can then sing with Isaac Watts, "Were the whole realm of nature mine, that were a present far too small; love so amazing, so divine, demands my soul, my life, my all."

STAND UP, STAND UP FOR JESUS

Stand up stand up for Jesus, ye soldiers of the cross;
Lift high his royal banner, it must not suffer loss.
From vict'ry unto vic'try, his army shall he lead,
Till every foe is vanquished and Christ is Lord indeed.

Stand up, stand up for Jesus, the trumpet call obey;
Forth to the mighty conflict, in this his glorious day.
Ye that are men, now serve him against unnumbered foes;
Let courage rise with danger and strength to strength oppose.

Stand up, stand up for Jesus, stand in his strength alone;
The arm of flesh will fail you, ye dare not trust your own.
Put on the gospel armor, each piece put on with prayer;
Where duty calls, or danger, be never wanting there.

Stand up, stand up for Jesus, the strife will not be long;
This day the noise of battle, the next the victor's song;
To him who overcometh, a crown of life shall be;
He, with the King of glory, shall reign eternally.

George Duffield Jr. (1818–1888)

CHAPTER 4

KEY PRINCIPLE FOUR: *CONTROLLED BY ONE MESSAGE*

Of this church I was made a minister . . . so that I might fully carry out the preaching of the word of God, that is, the mystery which has been hidden from the past ages and generations, but has now been manifested to His saints, to whom God willed to make known what is the riches of the glory of this mystery among the Gentiles, which is Christ in you, the hope of glory.

Colossians 1:25-26

The year 2017 was a remarkable year for millions of Christians as together we celebrated the 500th anniversary of the Protestant Reformation that rescued countless millions from the bewitching deceptions of Roman Catholicism. Initiated by Martin Luther's publication of the Ninety-five Theses in 1517, Western Christianity was suddenly confronted with the true gospel. The great divines of that day heralded the revelation of *Scripture alone*. They understood that salvation is by *grace alone*, through *faith alone*, in *Christ alone*, for the *glory of God alone*. These five foundational truths, known as the "Five Solas,"[27] became the rallying cry of the Protestant reformers in response to specific theological perversions taught by the Roman Catholic Church.

Unfortunately, the gospel is still under siege. In fact, five hundred years after the Protestant Reformation, it still needs to be rescued from Roman Catholicism. According to a Pew Research Center survey, 52 percent of Protestants in the United States say, "both good deeds and faith are needed to get into heaven, a historically Catholic belief."[28] Believing such a heresy condemns someone to destruction in eternal hell (Gal. 1:8).

But the gospel must also be rescued from many churches where it is so distorted it bears little resemblance to the true gospel. Perversions like the *prosperity gospel*, the *easy-believism gospel*, and the *felt-needs gospel* are now commonplace. People are not being warned about the offended holiness of God that causes his wrath to abide on sinners. They do not hear Paul's sermon on "righteousness, self-control and the judgment to come" that caused Felix to tremble (Acts 24:25).

Even many true believers express frustration concerning "needs-based preaching" that offers no spiritual nourishment to those who are starving for the glory and greatness of God. The life-changing power of expository preaching has been traded for the sugar high of cotton candy sermonettes that give a brief burst of emotional energy followed by a long crash of spiritual lethargy.

Many young pastors are more comfortable exegeting Hollywood movies than the inspired Word of God. The sacred desk has become the psychologist's couch and sermons nothing more than self-help seminars. Why? Because the gospel Jesus preached is considered archaic, divisive, and offensive. As a result, like the latest version of the *iPhone*, it continues to be reinvented to meet the demands of the consumer. But where there is no gospel, there is no repentance, no regeneration, no justification, no sanctification, no indwelling Spirit, no new nature, no true worship, and no eternal life! What remains is a *Christless* Christianity and churches filled with counterfeit Christians.

While these problems may seem insurmountable and unique to our postmodern culture, fundamentally they are no different than what Jesus and the apostles dealt with in the first century. The disease is sin, and the cure is the gospel—the one message that controlled the apostle Paul who said, "Of this church I was made a minister . . . so that I might fully carry out the preaching of the word of God, that is, the mystery which has been hidden from the past ages and generations, but has now been manifested to His saints" (Col. 1:25-26). This is the fourth key principle for effective ministry that we will examine in this chapter.

CONTROLLED BY ONE MESSAGE—THE GOSPEL

The regions of the first-century world where the gospel was first preached were dominated primarily by the Greek mystery religions, along with Judaism being a small minority. It would be impossible to conceive of a more hostile environment in which to preach the gospel and plant churches. But by God's grace and power, sinners were converted and the church exploded in growth. He empowered men who were *controlled by one message*, namely, *the unadorned, unadulterated gospel as revealed in the totality of Scripture*—men devoted to preaching the Word of God.

We see this clearly in Paul's testimony:

> *Of this church I was made a minister according*
> *to the stewardship from God bestowed on me*
> *for your benefit, so that I might fully carry*
> *out the preaching of the word of God, that is,*
> *the mystery which has been hidden from the*
> *past ages and generations, but has now been*
> *manifested to His saints, to whom God willed to*
> *make known what is the riches of the glory of*

> *this mystery among the Gentiles, which is Christ*
> *in you, the hope of glory.*
>
> *(Col. 1:25-27)*

This is a fascinating text, because in it we can see the doctrinal *content* of Paul's sermons, which included "the mystery which has been hidden from the *past* ages and generations, but has now been manifested to His saints," a subject church growth gurus would never recommend for evangelism because the "unchurched" would find it utterly boring and irrelevant. Obviously, Paul disagreed.

By "mystery" Paul is referring to spiritual truths in the New Testament that would have remained hidden had God not chosen to reveal them. As a steward of these mysteries, he preached "the mystery among the Gentiles; which is Christ in you, the hope of glory" (v. 27), referring to the surpassing riches of the indwelling Christ by the Holy Spirit (John 14:23; Rom. 8:9-10).

But these mysteries also included "the mystery of the gospel" (Eph. 6:19), "the mystery of Christ" (Eph. 3:8-12), "the great mystery concerning Christ and the church" (Eph. 5:22-33), the "mystery" that "we shall not all sleep, but we shall all be changed" (1 Cor. 15:51cf.; 1 Thess. 4:13-18), "the mystery of lawlessness" (2 Thess. 2:7, 9), the "mystery ... that a partial hardening has happened to Israel" (Rom. 11:25-36), and the mystery, "BABYLON THE GREAT, THE MOTHER OF HARLOTS AND OF THE ABOMINATIONS OF THE EARTH" (Rev. 17:5).

Sadly, very few preachers today share Paul's stewardship commitment to preach these "mysteries" concerning Christ in all his glory—mysteries which Paul said, "God bestowed on me for your benefit" (Col. 1:25). I have talked with many believers who know virtually nothing about these magnificent truths, and worse yet, many do not care to hear them. Many professing Christians today are like the self-deceived Israelites who came to Jeremiah under the pretense of wanting to know the truth of God, promising "Whether it is pleasant or unpleasant, we will listen to the voice of the LORD our God" (Jer. 42:6). But once they learned what God would have them do, they became more obstinate and defiant than before, further away than ever from obeying the command of God (Jer. 43:1, 2; 44:16, 17).

Paul expands upon his responsibility further in his letter to the Corinthians: "But we speak the wisdom of God in a mystery, the hidden wisdom which God ordained before the ages for our glory" (1 Cor. 2:7). His use of the strong adversative conjunction "but" (Greek: *alla*) underscores the extreme contrast between man's wisdom and "God's wisdom" which is in an emphatic position in the Greek text, emphasizing both supernatural *possession* and *source*; it belongs *to* him and it comes *from* him.

This is further demonstrated through his use of the term "mystery" (Greek: *musterion*), which does not refer to some secret, mystical, enigmatic philosophy only known by certain elite initiates. As mentioned earlier, it describes *that which has been kept secret in the past and cannot be known until God reveals it*, referring to the revealed will and purposes of God given to all believers in the New Testament, namely, *the gospel*. He also calls it "the hidden wisdom of God" because it is the secret wisdom that God intentionally conceals from the natural man (1 Cor. 2:14), who prefers earthly wisdom to God's wisdom. It is this wisdom, "God's wisdom," that we are to preach with confidence, knowing it was "ordained before the ages for our glory" (v. 7).

As pastors, we have a stewardship responsibility to proclaim these mysteries and all the associated truths surrounding them, each being woven throughout the tapestry of Scripture. Like Paul, we need to be *controlled by one message*, which requires a commitment to the systematic, in-depth preaching, teaching, and application of the Word, as Paul put it, "declaring ... the whole purpose of God" (Eph. 20:27). This eliminates watered-down, dumbed-down, needs-based, entertainment preaching to the unsaved—preaching that is far different from biblical preaching that is both convicting and edifying. The legacy of weak pulpits is catastrophic. The primary reason the church makes so little difference in the world today is because too many pulpits are filled with entrepreneurs, entertainers, therapists, and political activists rather than "stewards of the mysteries of God."

MESSAGE DETERMINES STRATEGY

Paul's commitment to being a trustworthy steward of the mysteries of God dictated his *strategy* in gospel ministry. This can be seen in his testimony to the saints in Corinth, an exceedingly decadent, idolatrous—yet sophisticated—city. In his first epistle to the Corinthians, we gain insight into the strategy he used when he first approached that pagan culture. And what is particularly fascinating is that his confidence in the message he preached produced a philosophy of ministry that could only be described as *counterintuitive.* The Corinthians had never heard or seen anything like Paul. They thought he was a complete moron (1 Cor. 1:23). He certainly did not pack out the local amphitheater with crowds of people who were coming to listen to him.

The common manner of proclamation they were accustomed to was the flowery rhetoric of worldly-wise philosophers, skilled orators able to present man's perceived wisdom in ways that were both appealing and compelling. It was basically a form of entertainment for the masses. People would even align themselves according to sectarian parties that supported their favorite philosopher (a divisive spirit new converts carried with them into the church that caused disunity). Through their oratory powers, philosophers would sway the naïve and ignorant crowds to believe what they taught, not so much on the basis of *what* they said, but *how* they said it—a common phenomenon of manipulation used by many preachers and politicians today.

So you would think that, to be effective, gospel preachers would employ the same strategy and study such techniques, and cultivate eloquence and the art of persuasion; they would adopt a manner, a style, and demeanor that would fit the culture—otherwise no one would listen! You would think Paul would have said, "I must let the culture shape my delivery and then align the content of my message with the spirit of the age; I must endear myself to them in creative ways, start a conversation, find some common ground, then I can capture their attention and induce them to exercise their will to make a decision for Christ."

But because he embraced a biblical soteriology, Paul's *message was uncompromising* and his *manner was unconventional.* His strategies for church growth made no sense from the world's perspective. Remember, his message is summarized in one powerful statement: "For I determined to know nothing among you except Jesus Christ, and Him crucified" (1 Cor. 2:2). He understood what many today seem to forget, and that is, the message of the gospel is the only message God uses to save souls and bring glory to himself. Though it is a stumbling block to the Jews and foolishness to the Greeks, "to those who are the called, both Jews and Greeks," it is "Christ the power of God and the wisdom of God" (1 Cor. 1:23, 24).

The phrase, "Christ, and Him crucified" refers to the complete, unadulterated gospel with all its offense—which includes the entirety of God's revelation to man found in Scripture. Everything else is a waste of time. Although "the word of the cross is foolishness to those who are perishing . . . to us who are being saved it is the power of God" (1 Cor. 1:18). Everything else is the mere *wisdom of men*, which God has promised to destroy (v. 19). Man's most erudite philosophies and clever religious systems have no more ability to save the souls of men than a spit in the river has in changing its course. The gospel alone is "the power of God for salvation, to the Jew first and also to the Greek" (Rom. 1:16).

What a tragedy to hear what comes out of so many evangelical pulpits these days—frivolous drivel with the depth of frost on a pumpkin. When I was growing up in the 1960s I remember hearing the phrase, "God has a wonderful plan for your life!" which translates into, "Jesus died so you can have a happy, successful, and prosperous life"—a dangerous distortion of the true gospel. The same ear-tickling error has made "The Purpose Driven Life" movement so appealing. Then there's "The Prosperity Gospel," and the pernicious "Carnal Christian" gospel that insists individuals can be Christians yet remain indistinguishable in their lifestyles from the people among whom they live (Eph. 4:17-22).

Sadly, the camel's nose of culture was allowed to enter the tent of the church in the "seeker sensitive" movement, so it should be no surprise that he continues to force his way in completely. Once inside, he will trample the gospel underfoot, destroy all that brings glory to Christ, and exalt himself as the one to be worshipped. This would be Satan's greatest triumph!

The common denominator of all perverted gospels is that

they make *people's felt-needs* the center of gravity around which God's plan of redemption must orbit. With God playing second fiddle, *man* distorts the message of the gospel and creates what Jesus described as a wide gate and broad way "that leads to destruction, and many are those who enter by it" (Matt. 7:14).

Because of his absolute confidence in the supernatural power of divine truth and the Spirit's power to raise the spiritually dead, Paul's only concern was being bold enough to unleash the truth of the gospel without compromise. In fact, this was such a great apprehension that he asked the saints in Ephesus to

> *pray on my behalf, that utterance may be given*
> *to me in the opening of my mouth, to make*
> *known with boldness the mystery of the gospel,*
> *for which I am an ambassador in chains; that*
> *in proclaiming it I may speak boldly, as I ought*
> *to speak.*
>
> *(Eph. 6:19-20)*

Paul's strategy was simple: preach nothing else "except Jesus Christ, and Him crucified" (1 Cor. 2:2). Now this doesn't mean all he ever preached was evangelistic messages on the atonement. Not at all. We learn from Acts 18:11 that during the year and a half that he ministered in Corinth, he "taught the word of God among them." But whenever Paul preached, Christ was always the primary focus and the gospel was the ultimate answer to every human problem.

Notice how his uncompromising message determined his unconventional manner in Corinth:

> *And when I came to you, brethren, I did not*
> *come with superiority of speech or of wisdom,*
> *proclaiming to you the testimony of God. For*
> *I determined to know nothing among you*
> *except Jesus Christ, and Him crucified. I was*
> *with you in weakness and in fear and in much*
> *trembling, and my message and my preaching*
> *were not in persuasive words of wisdom, but in*
> *demonstration of the Spirit and of power, so that*

your faith would not rest on the wisdom of men,
but on the power of God.

(1 Cor. 2:1-5)

Paul saw no need to mimic the style and rhetoric of the philosophers. He knew it was the *Word preached* and not the *preacher of the Word* that really mattered. In his own inimitable style, Spurgeon put it this way:

> *The power that is in the Gospel does not lie in the eloquence of the preacher, otherwise men would be the converters of souls, nor does it lie in the preacher's learning, otherwise it would consist in the wisdom of men. We might preach until our tongues rotted, till we would exhaust our lungs and die, but never a soul would be converted unless the Holy Spirit be with the Word of God to give it the power to convert the soul.[29]*

Can't you just see Paul in Corinth? Can't you just see the look on the people's faces when they heard him speak and really listened to what he was saying? He described their reaction to his gospel message this way: "To Jews a stumbling block, and to Gentiles foolishness, but to those who are the called, both Jews and Greeks, Christ the power of God and the wisdom of God. Because the foolishness of God is wiser than men, and the weakness of God is stronger than men" (1 Cor. 1:23-25). The apostle Paul rightly believed that only the gospel can make people right with God, transform their hearts, free them from the bondage of sin, empower them with the indwelling Holy Spirit, and give them eternal glory.

DOCTRINAL PREACHING AND PRAYER

The New Testament makes it clear that *doctrinal preaching* bathed in *prayer* is what God has ordained for the growth of his church.

First, consider the matter of doctrinal preaching (which will be examined more thoroughly in the next chapter). This is what Paul had in mind when he said, "Of *this church* I was made a minister . . . so that I might fully carry out the *preaching of* the word of God" (Col. 1:25); he "did not shrink from declaring . . . the whole purpose of God" (Acts 20:27). We also see doctrinal preaching in the ministry of John the Baptist (Matt. 3:1), Jesus (Matt. 4:17), Peter (Acts 2:14-36), Stephen (Acts 7:2-53), and Paul (Acts 28:31) who exhorted Timothy to do the same, that is, "preach the Word" (2 Tim. 4:2; cf. 1 Tim. 4:16). Throughout the New Testament we see theological, doctrinal content being the *sine qua non* of preaching, with the message of the gospel being the dominant theme.

Consider the content of Peter's evangelistic gospel sermon at Pentecost. There he unpacked the prophecies of Joel that pointed to Jesus the Nazarene as the Messiah of Israel. And unlike many preachers today, he did not shy away from the doctrine of the sovereignty of God. Without the slightest equivocation, he told his audience that the atoning work of Christ on the cross was according to God's predetermined plan ordained in eternity past. With boldness he declared, "This *Man*, delivered over by the predetermined plan and foreknowledge of God, you nailed to a cross by the hands of godless men and put *Him* to death" (Acts 2:23).

He went on to say, "Let all the house of Israel know for certain that God has made Him both Lord and Christ—this Jesus whom you crucified" (Acts 2:36). So much for being *seeker sensitive*! In the course of his sermon he also exposited David's words pertaining to the Messiah, and exegeted Psalm 16 where the Lord spoke of his resurrection prophetically (which clearly proved that Jesus Christ, not David, would be raised to reign). And what was the result? Luke answers:

> *Now when they heard this, they were pierced to*
> *the heart, and said to Peter and the rest of the*
> *apostles, "Brethren, what shall we do?" Peter said*
> *to them, "Repent, and each of you be baptized*
> *in the name of Jesus Christ for the forgiveness*
> *of your sins; and you will receive the gift of the*
> *Holy Spirit" . . . And with many other words he*
> *solemnly testified and kept on exhorting them,*
> *saying, "Be saved from this perverse generation!"*
> *(Acts 2:37-40)*

Luke went on to describe the priorities of their worship: "They were continually devoting themselves to the apostles' teaching and to fellowship, to the breaking of bread and to prayer" (v. 42). The term "devoted" (a form of *proskartereo*) carries the idea of *steadfast dedication* and *persevering affection*—virtues the unsaved do not share. In every recorded gospel proclamation, the content of their instruction included expositions of the Old Testament, teachings from the life and ministry of Jesus, and new revelation given by the Holy Spirit to the apostles. This is how God causes his church to grow.

I fear, however, that in their search for the right formula to attract a crowd, many pastors have neglected the divine means of growing a church. Instead, they have sold their birthright for a mess of pottage. Unlike Paul, too many preachers are not controlled by one message: "the preaching of the word of God" (Col. 1:25)—at the heart of which is the gospel of God. Few seem to understand the importance of synthesizing the great doctrines of biblical soteriology with all the other magnificent doctrines of Scripture for which we are exhorted to "contend earnestly" (Jude 3). Sadly, *contending earnestly* is now being defined by some evangelical leaders as creating a hostile environment that is injurious to the gospel. Such an errant position will continue to produce unimaginable forms of moral and religious compromise.

Realizing this danger, the apostle Paul said, "I am under compulsion; for woe is me if I do not preach the gospel" (1 Cor. 9:16). He understood that sinners must be confronted with great doctrinal truths, like the sovereignty of God and his offended holiness, the sinfulness of sin, the certain judgment of God, the brevity of life, the glory of the person and work of Christ, and the promise of resurrection. The preacher must help sinners probe their hearts with brutal honesty to determine whether or not they have a personal conviction of sin and a proper relationship with the living God, because he knows the unadulterated gospel is the only message God uses to raise the spiritually dead to everlasting life. Jesus made it clear: *a compromised gospel will deceive the many, and it will never save the few* (Matt. 7:13-27). The clear, precise, and distinguishing marks of a true Christianity versus a false Christianity must be clearly defined, especially today where the line of demarcation between what *is* and *is not* Christian has been virtually eradicated.

Second, it is important to understand the indispensable role of prayer in relation to preaching. I find it quite telling that popular church growth strategies underemphasize fervent prayer in preaching, and most do not mention it at all. When was the last time a pastor's conference was devoted to prayer in preaching? Minimizing the need for prayer betrays the underlying deception that continues to rob the church of its power, namely, the belief that *man's methods can produce conversions and even revival*—a misconception that both Scripture and history prove to be false. Intercessory prayer, which shows our dependency upon God and concern for others, is a striking feature seen in all the New Testament epistles. It is the indispensable discipline of prayer that unleashes unfathomable spiritual power that alone can accomplish what man can never do.

Jesus is our supreme example. Although he was God incarnate, prayer was vital to his preaching. He understood his utter dependence upon the Father and the Holy Spirit to carry out such a task. For this reason Luke records how "Jesus Himself would *often* slip away to the wilderness and pray" (Luke 5:16). It was only after "He spent the whole night in prayer to God" (Luke 6:12) that he preached his great sermon on the plain (vv. 20-49). Prayer preceded his announcement concerning the church temporarily replacing Israel as the new custodian of truth and possessing the keys of the kingdom (Matt. 16:18-19; Luke 9:18). Only after prayer did Jesus announce his impending death and resurrection, the priority of self-denial, the danger of self-promotion, the judgment for those who are ashamed of Christ, and the certain promise of his glorious return (Luke 9:18, 22-27). Given Jesus' priority in prayer, we must guard against any sense of self-sufficiency that might minimize our need to remain in a spirit of prayer.

Did not Jesus say, "Ask, and it will be given to you; seek, and you will find; knock, and it will be opened to you" (Matt. 7:7)? Did he not also promise, "All things you ask in prayer, believing, you shall receive" (21:22)? Has not the apostle John told us, "Now this is the confidence that we have in Him, that if we ask anything according to His will, He hears us" (1 John 5:14)? Obviously, prayer is to be a priority, especially in our preaching.

THE GROWING GAP BETWEEN THE CHURCH AND THE UNCHURCHED

Unfortunately, but not unexpectedly, there is a growing gap between what is commonly referred to as the "churched" and the "unchurched" (those who claim to be Christians but do not attend worship services). While a small percentage of the *unchurched* are just worldly, spiritually immature believers, *most are unsaved*, "Christian" in name only. Jesus warned about this when he described "the few" who would *even find*, much less *enter* the narrow gate of genuine repentance; in contrast to "the many" who will enter through "the wide gate" and travel the broad way that leads to destruction (Matt. 7:13-14). Jesus went on to add, "Not everyone who says to Me, 'Lord, Lord,' will enter the kingdom of heaven, but he who does the will of My Father who is in heaven *will enter*" (Matt. 7:21). It is likely, therefore, that most of the *unchurched* fit into that sorrowful category of self-deception (as do most of the "churched.")

Jesus made it clear that the litmus test of genuine saving faith is doing "the will of [the] Father," which includes many things revealed in Scripture, especially having a passionate desire to know, love, serve, and worship him. The truly regenerate will *want* to do this. It will be the joy of their heart—not a *duty* but a *desire*. True Christians will *want* to be shepherded by godly men; they will *want* to grow in the grace and knowledge of Christ and fellowship with other believers. At the moment of salvation, Christ places every true believer into his body, the church, by the Holy Spirit, who then takes up residence in that person (1 Cor. 12:13). So, naturally, they will *want* to be a part of that living organism to which they now belong. They will *want* "to stimulate one another to love and good deeds, not forsaking our own assembling together, as is the habit of some" (Heb. 10:24-25). Anyone with no interest in these things has no basis to claim genuine saving faith. Rather than calling them *unchurched*, it would be more accurate to sorrowfully refer to them as *unsaved*.

But this is not a tenable position with churches that cater to the *unchurched*. Once again, those holding to this terminology assume the *unchurched* are true believers who merely find church boring, irrelevant, and unnecessary. This can be seen in the underlying premise of an article on this topic from *The*

Barna Group that reads in part: "Based upon more than 2 decades of tracking research, *The Barna Group* has discovered real and significant shifts in unchurched attitudes, assumptions, allegiances and behaviors." The article went on to describe five trends (I have only listed the headings):

1. Secularization is on the rise.

2. People are less open to the idea of church.

3. Churchgoing is no longer mainstream.

4. There are different expectations of church involvement.

5. There is skepticism about churches' contributions to society.[30]

In light of this research, David Kinnamen, president of *Barna Group* and co-editor, with George Barna, of the new book *Churchless*, from which this data is taken, says: "How can we recapture an urgency to fulfill the Great Commission while treating our churchless friends with respect?" He goes on to suggest, "Wrestling with answers to this question will help prepare a faith community to engage more meaningfully with unchurched people."[31]

So how can we show respect, and love for "our churchless friends"? What should we do to reach them? The biblical answer is straightforward. We must do the same thing Jesus and the apostles did: *preach "Jesus Christ, and Him crucified"* (1 Cor. 2:2, emphasis mine).

"But," says the critic, "given the growing gap between the *churched* and the *unchurched*, it would appear that old message isn't working in this culture and we must do things differently." Wrong! In most cases the "old message" isn't even being preached. But where it is, it is working precisely as God has planned. It may not be filling churches and packing stadiums, but numerical growth is never God's measure of success. Never once in the New Testament record do we see any praise offered to a church because it was growing in numbers. We are also warned that there will be seasons in which the mass of professing Christians will not endure sound doctrine (2 Tim. 4:3, 4), and perhaps, like never before, we are there!

What we must understand is that *every single person God has elected to salvation is being saved at the precise moment he decreed.* Jesus made this clear when he said, "All that the Father gives Me *shall* come to Me" (John 6:37; emphasis added); like the elect in Corinth of whom we read, "as many as had been appointed to eternal life believed" (Acts 13:48). We can have absolute confidence in God's sovereign election in salvation "because God has chosen [us] from the beginning for salvation through sanctification by the Spirit and faith in the truth" (2 Thess. 2:13). He is the One who "chose us in Him before the foundation of the world, that we should be holy and blameless before Him" (Eph. 1:4).

So while we must never be passive or indifferent, there is no need to be alarmed about the growing gap between the *churched* and the *unchurched.* Christ has promised, "I will build My church" (Matt. 16:18). We must never assume there is some deficiency in the gospel requiring us to customize it so it will overcome the latest version of cultural resistance. The unregenerate have always hated the Word because they hate Christ and all who belong to him (John 15:18-19). Notwithstanding their inevitable antipathy, "faith" still "comes by hearing, and hearing by the Word of Christ" (Rom. 10:17). We must never forget that the faithful preaching of God's Word *has* and *will continue* to either harden or soften human hearts— one or the other. God himself has affirmed this through his prophet Isaiah:

> *For as the rain and the snow come down from*
> *heaven, and do not return there without watering*
> *the earth and making it bear and sprout, and*
> *furnishing seed to the sower and bread to the*
> *eater; so will My word be which goes forth*
> *from My mouth; it will not return to Me empty,*
> *without accomplishing what I desire, and without*
> *succeeding in the matter for which I sent it.*
>
> *(Isa. 55:10-11)*

It is the assurance of this glorious promise that animates the heart of every faithful pastor when he stands behind a pulpit with his Bible open and says, "Thus says the Lord!" We must sow the true gospel seed, not some artificial hybrid advertised to grow in any soil. Then we pray for God to do what only he can do in causing it to germinate in the fertile soil of every heart he has prepared by his electing love. Firmly anchored in the Rock of Gibraltar of sovereign grace, we then have total confidence that God will accomplish all he has purposed. For "we have obtained an inheritance, having been predestined according to His purpose who works all things after the counsel of His will" (Eph. 1:11).

When addressing an audience, we never know who among the unsaved are the elect of God. But undoubtedly some are there, even among the most hostile crowds. Some of us were once among the scoffers, yet God saved us. This reality should embolden every minister of the Word. Like the situation in Corinth where the Lord encouraged Paul saying, "Do not be afraid *any longer*, but go on speaking and do not be silent; for I am with you, and no man will attack you in order to harm you, *for I have many people in this city*" (Acts 18:9-10; emphasis added).

THE GROWING GAP PROPHESIED

The steady decline in fundamental, Bible-believing church attendance is consistent with the metastasizing corruption of sin and the promised accumulation of deceptions and false teachers that will characterize the end of human history (2 Tim. 3:1). With the rise of secularization and religious pluralism, many so-called Christians now reject the claim that Scripture is the inspired, inerrant, infallible, authoritative, all-sufficient Word of God. So they have no spiritual authority other than their own opinions derived from the darkened understanding of the flesh and Satan's diabolical world system. As a result, they prefer a new kind of spirituality—one that rejects the revelation of God, especially the doctrine of salvation. The idea of a Father sacrificing his Son on a cross to appease his wrath is considered barbaric and utterly inconsistent with what Jesus taught.

And perhaps the most offensive is the doctrine of human depravity which states that human beings are sinners by nature and under the condemnation of a holy God who will send them to hell unless they repent and trust in Christ as Savior. Increasing numbers of people who call themselves "Christian" consider this to be utterly preposterous. But this is to be expected of the spiritually dead (Eph. 2:1) who are as unresponsive to spiritual truth as a corpse in a casket (Rom. 8:7-8; 1 Cor. 2:14; 2 Cor. 4:4; Eph. 4:17-18). Only the divine miracle of regeneration can recreate sinners and make them alive to God (2 Cor. 4:6). And what a magnificent miracle that is to behold!

Add to all this the tsunami of moral sewage and every conceivable spiritual deception flowing through the Internet, it is no wonder there is a growing resentment toward the things of God. No wonder there is a decline and morphing of the Christian church into something it was never intended to be. By compromising the message of the gospel to somehow stem the tide of resistance, churches have ceased being the church. As a result, they have forfeited the Spirit's power and operate in the flesh. Apostate churches like that at Laodicea (Rev. 3:14-22), and apostate individuals (Heb. 10:25-31; 2 Peter 2:20-22) have always existed, and apostasy (a deliberate and total abandonment of the faith previously held)[32] will continue to intensify as the world is being prepared for the Antichrist and "the apostasy" he will commit (2 Thess. 2:3). Paul's use of the definite article ("the apostasy") indicates a specific act of apostasy that will be committed by "the man of lawlessness" who will be "revealed, the son of destruction, who opposes and exalts himself above every so-called god or object of worship, so that he takes his seat in the temple of God, displaying himself as being God" (vv. 3-4).

But prior to this unprecedented act of blasphemy that will occur during the pre-kingdom judgments just prior to our Lord's return, conditions will continue to deteriorate. The gap between the *churched* and the *unchurched* will continue to grow. And if you consider the fact that most ostensibly Christian churches today are not *true* New Testament churches and are populated by more tares than wheat, the present gap is even greater than reported. Paul warned about this when he said,

> *But realize this, that in the last days difficult times will come. For men will be lovers of self, lovers of money, boastful, arrogant, revilers, disobedient to parents, ungrateful, unholy, unloving, irreconcilable, malicious gossips, without self-control, brutal, haters of good, treacherous, reckless, conceited, lovers of*

pleasure rather than lovers of God, holding to
a form of godliness, although they have denied
its power; Avoid such men as these. For among
them are those who enter into households and
captivate weak women weighed down with sins,
led on by various impulses, always learning and
never able to come to the knowledge of the truth.
(2 Tim. 3:1-7)

Prior to Christ's return, things will not get better and better; they will grow worse and worse. No reasonable and informed person would deny the growing hostility toward Bible-believing Christians in the United States. In fact, persecution is on the rise around the world. Paul warned, "But evil men and impostors will proceed *from bad* to worse, deceiving and being deceived" (2 Tim. 3:12-13). In his Olivet Discourse in Matthew 24, Jesus warned that the period immediately prior to his return will be characterized by persecution, apostasy, and unbelief. Paul also warned of this saying, "All who desire to live godly in Christ Jesus will be persecuted" (2 Tim. 3:12).

Jesus also predicted that true faith will be very rare when he returns, as implied in his question, "When the Son of Man comes, will He find faith on the earth?" (Luke 18:8). The rarity of genuine faith that will exist in the world when Christ returns is seen even more dramatically in Jesus' prophecy in Luke 17:26 where he states: "Just as it was in the days of Noah, so will it be in the days of the Son of man." Talk about a gap between the *churched* and the *unchurched*! Notwithstanding the vast numbers of people who inhabited the earth in the days of Noah, only eight were faithful. Only eight were rescued from the waters of divine judgment.

Despite all this, never once are we commanded to change our message. Even during the final days of the outpouring of God's wrath upon the world that utterly despises Christ during the tribulation judgments just prior to his return, the "the eternal gospel" will be proclaimed by an angelic messenger:

And I saw another angel flying in midheaven,
*having an **eternal gospel** to preach to those who*
live on the earth, and to every nation and tribe and

tongue and people; and he said with a loud voice,
"Fear God, and give Him glory, because the hour of
His judgment has come; worship Him who made the
heaven and the earth and sea and springs of waters.
(Rev. 14:6-7, emphasis mine)

Final Word

Because he was first *consumed with God's glory*—the first key principle for effective ministry—the apostle Paul was *content with his suffering, convinced of his calling,* and *controlled by one message,* "Christ, and Him crucified." This naturally requires a passionate commitment to understanding and explaining the gospel message revealed by God on every page of Scripture. Because of this, Paul was also *confident with one method: doctrinal preaching.* This cannot be done apart from the faithful exposition of the Word, the fifth key principle for effective ministry, affirmed in the next chapter.

OH, FOR A THOUSAND TONGUES TO SING

Oh, for a thousand tongues to sing
My great Redeemer's praise,
The glories of my God and king,
The triumphs of His grace!

My gracious Master and my God,
Assist me to proclaim,
To spread through all the earth abroad,
The honors of Thy name.

Jesus! the name that charms our fears,
That bids our sorrows cease—
'Tis music in the sinner's ears,
'Tis life, and health, and peace.

He breaks the pow'r of canceled sin,
He sets the pris'ner free;
His blood can make the foulest clean,
His blood availed for me.

He speaks, and, list'ning to His voice,
New life the dead receive,
The mournful, broken hearts rejoice,
The humble poor believe.

Glory to God, and praise and love
Be ever, ever giv'n
By saints below and saints above,
The church in earth and heav'n.

Charles Wesley (1707–1788)

CHAPTER 5

KEY PRINCIPLE FIVE:
CONFIDENT WITH ONE METHOD

*"And we proclaim Him, admonishing every man
and teaching every man with all wisdom."*

Colossians 1:28

Sometime during the early years of my ministry, I read a very informative book (every preacher must read) written by John MacArthur, Jr., and the faculty of The Master's Seminary entitled, *Rediscovering Expository Preaching: Balancing the Science and Art of Biblical Exposition*. In that work I read a statement written by an unknown parishioner that accurately underscored the solemn responsibility of biblical preaching, and offered a plan on how to be effective to that end. The writer said this:

Fling him into his office. Tear the "Office" sign from the door and nail on the sign, "Study." Take him off the mailing list. Lock him up with his books and his typewriter and his Bible. Slam him down on his knees before texts and broken hearts and the flock of lives of a superficial flock and a holy God.

Force him to be the one man in our surfeited communities who knows about God. Throw him into the ring to box with God until he learns how short his arms are. Engage him to wrestle with God all the night through. And let him come out only when he's bruised and beaten into being a blessing.

Shut his mouth forever spouting remarks, and stop his tongue forever tripping lightly over every nonessential. Require him to have something to say before he dares break the silence. Bend his knees in the lonesome valley.

Burn his eyes with weary study. Wreck his emotional poise with worry for God. And make him exchange his pious stance for a humble walk with God and man. Make him spend and be spent for the glory of God. Rip out his telephone. Burn up his ecclesiastical success sheets. Put water in his gas tank. Give him a Bible and tie him to the pulpit. And make him preach the Word of the living God!

Test him. Quiz him. Examine him. Humiliate him for his ignorance of things divine. Shame him for his good comprehension of finances, batting averages, and political infighting. Laugh at his frustrated effort to play psychiatrist. Form a choir and raise a chant and haunt him with it night and day—"Sir, we would see Jesus."

When at long last he dares assay the pulpit, ask him if he has a word from God. If he does not, then dismiss him. Tell him you can read the morning paper and digest the television commentaries, and think through the day's superficial problems, and manage the community's weary drives, and bless the sordid baked potatoes and green beans, ad infinitum, better than he can.

Command him not to come back until he's read and reread, written and rewritten, until he can stand up, worn and forlorn, and say, "Thus saith the Lord." Break him across the board of his ill-gotten popularity. Smack him hard with his own prestige. Corner him with questions about God. Cover him with demands for celestial wisdom. And give him no escape until he's back against the wall of the Word.

And sit down before him and listen to the only word he has left—God's Word. Let him be totally ignorant of the down street gossip, but give him a chapter and order him to walk around it, camp on it, sup with it, and come at last to speak it backward and forward, until all he says about it rings with the truth of eternity.

And when he's burned out by the flaming Word, when he's consumed at last by the fiery grace blazing through him, and when he's privileged to translate the truth of God to man, finally transferred from earth to heaven, then bear him away gently and blow a muted trumpet and lay him down softly. Place a two-edged sword in his coffin, and raise the tomb triumphant. For he was a brave soldier of the Word. And ere he died, he had become a man of God.[33]

I have read and reread that admonition many times. It perfectly captures the essence of the serious nature of pastoral ministry set forth in the New Testament and summarized in Paul's testimony to the Colossians, where he says,

We proclaim Him, admonishing every man and teaching every man with all wisdom, so that we may present every man complete in Christ. For this purpose also I labor, striving according to His power, which mightily works within me.

(Col. 1:28-29)

That parishioner's insightful plan motivated me to have a portion of it inscribed on a piece of brass that adorns the inner shelf of my pulpit to this very day. It is positioned at the top where it can be easily seen. The inscription reads: "*We would see Jesus.*" Whenever I read this I am reminded of the proper attitude necessary to be a faithful steward of the mysteries of God. Preaching is to put the glory of *Christ* on display, not to draw attention to the preacher. John the Baptist said it best: "He must increase, but I must decrease" (John 3:30). Like Paul, who was "determined to know nothing among you except Jesus Christ, and Him crucified" (1 Cor. 2:2), we proclaim the glory of the Son, the incarnate Word, the pre-existent, self-existent, uncreated Creator of the universe—the divine *logos* (John 1:1), "the true light which, coming into the world, enlightens every man" (v. 9). And this simply cannot be done apart from the systematic, in-depth, doctrinal preaching, teaching, and application of the Word. Without question, the apostle Paul was *confident with this one method.*

Unless preachers believe this with all their heart, they have no business standing behind a pulpit. Apart from the faithful proclamation of *divine truth*—a conviction worth dying for—they will have no authority and no power, and the church will continue to lose what little influence it has left on our postmodern world and on believers who are not used to hearing it, much less obeying it. As preachers of the gospel, we must never forget this.

PAUL, THE MASTER EXPOSITOR

The apostle Paul was a master Bible expositor. His epistles are essentially Bible expositions. Unlike the superficial "sermonettes for Christianettes" that typically pass for preaching these days, he unleashed the Word of God with compelling clarity and set the first century ablaze with the gospel.

The term "exposit" literally means *to expound or explain in a detailed manner.* Expository preaching is therefore a doctrinal proclamation of the Word of God derived from an exegetical process that is concerned only with the revelation of God, not the wisdom of man. Therefore it carefully conveys the God-intended meaning of a text, which will be linked to other great doctrines and theological truths. Then, when the text has been accurately explained, the preacher will passionately apply its meaning to the contemporary issues of life.

Unfortunately, pastors devoted to preaching sound doctrine seem to be a dying breed. Sadly, evangelicalism has gradually been swept away by the current of a postmodern culture that wants nothing to do with moral absolutes or authoritarian truth claims. In an effort to be appealing, it continues to jettison anything that smacks of dogmatism, especially doctrinal preaching. D.A. Carson makes this observation:

> *Over the last few years there has been a major push to abandon expository preaching for what is loosely called "narrative" preaching. The diagnosis goes something like this: These are postmodern times, marked by the collapse of confidence in the Enlightenment project and a rational certainty about "truth." So now hearers are more intuitive than logical; they are reached more through images and stories than through propositions and principles. They are also allergic to authoritarian declarations. We must adapt to the less rational, non-authoritarian, narrative-hungry sensibilities of our time.[34]*

Yielding to the culture is always a dangerous proposition, with many unintended consequences for the church. Inevitably, the authority of Scripture is the first thing to go. *Sola Scriptura* is replaced by *sola cultura*, as Os Guinness quipped. Gone are reverent worship services where people know they are entering into the presence of an infinitely holy God. Gone, too, is any focus on the majesty of God revealed in his Word. Slick entrepreneurs with sufficient panache to attract the subjective and individualistic culture have largely replaced great Bible expositors. Doctrine is out; relativism is in. But what is really ironic is this: *the entrepreneurs who have tried to make the church more relevant to the culture by selling a spirituality disconnected to biblical truth have instead made it utterly irrelevant.* Even the most arrogant, politically correct, morally bankrupt, millennial snowflake can spot a superficial, worthless, phony religious sideshow when they see one—no matter how good the band and or delicious the coffee.

Can there be any better illustration of this than the Bill

Hybels, Willow Creek Community Church experiment? David Wells addresses this in his book, *The Courage to Be Protestant: Reformation Faith in Today's World*. Here's his analysis of what happened:

Hybels made a rather stunning discovery after he had been in business for a while. Using a tool from the business-consulting world, over 11,000 past and present members of Willow Creek, which he founded, were surveyed in 2004 and again in 2007. The survey included six other churches. The results were published in Reveal: Where Are You? in 2007.

Hybels was shocked to find that there was no correlation between the growing numbers he was seeing at Willow Creek and evidence that they were maturing in their faith. In fact, attendance in church had little impact on their love of God and others. At least, that is what they said. Hybels concluded that church had had an important role for many at the beginning of their spiritual life but this importance tailed off as they moved along. Church, it turned out, was a place to start but not really a place to stay in.

It was, I think, a devastating finding. The Hybels experiment was producing pygmies unless they took matters into their own hands and sought growth without the help of the church. But are we surprised? Who could seriously imagine that the kind of slick business approach, the let-us-fit-our-message-into-your-busy-schedule mentality, would have produced anything else? Of course the Christianity that results from this kind of thing is going to be small, shrunken, cramped, and limited. It will not be able to command how life is to be lived in our complex, harsh, and highly demanding world.

This is always the rub in this kind of experiment. The form greatly modifies the content. The music may be professional, the service conveniently short, the skits and plays ever so professionally done, but this form actually undercuts the seriousness of the faith. In this marketing world the form, of course, is actually the product, pretty much the only product. The "product" is not really the faith. It is the packaging in which that faith is supposed to come. But the form replaces the content or "product." In this market the sale has to be done quickly and as painlessly as possible because the customers have itchy feet. That greatly militates against the depth any church can have. And that is why a deep chasm opened up between the church marketers and historic Protestant orthodoxy. It is less that the truths of this orthodoxy were being assailed than that they seemed to be irrelevant to the building of the church. More than that, they seemed to stand in the way of its success.[35]

As pastors, with our love for Christ and his great commission animating our hearts, we all want to reach the lost with the gospel and teach believers to obey all the Lord commands. We know firsthand the life-transforming power of saving grace. But we must be careful. We must look beyond the tech-savvy, entertainment addicted, truth-hating, self-absorbed, narcissistic mindset of our culture, and remember that these people struggle with all the misery associated with their sin and the God-hating world they love. We live amongst them; some attend our church. We must love them, pray for them, and give them the gospel. They are hurting, confused, frustrated, angry, depressed, addicted, lonely, disconnected. You name it; they struggle with it. Although they are too blind to see it, they need Christ and him crucified. And it is our responsibility to give them a taste of the glory that could be theirs.

THE BATTLE FOR THE MIND

The mind is clearly the battlefield upon which we must fight. In evangelism we must remember, "The god of this world has blinded the minds of the unbelievers, to keep them from seeing the light of the gospel of the glory of Christ, who is the image of God" (2 Cor. 4:4). There is perhaps no greater example of this than in the new spirituality of our postmodern world, where in the United States, "80 percent believe that a person should arrive at his or her own beliefs independent of any external authority such as a church. Indeed, 60 percent say that since we all have God within us, churches are unnecessary."[36]

While the natural mind is darkened in understanding (Eph. 4:18), even the renewed mind is vulnerable to Satan's fiery darts (Eph. 6:16; 2 Cor. 11:3). Think of the never-ending deceptions that lead believers into miserable places they themselves would never have chosen. For this reason, Peter offers a strong admonition: "Therefore, prepare your minds for action, keep sober in spirit, fix your hope completely on the grace to be brought to you at the revelation of Jesus Christ" (1 Peter 1:13).

Needless to say, our great adversary the devil (1 Peter 5:8), "the father of lies" (John 8:44) is always competing with anyone who dares to proclaim the truth. Despite all the benefits of electronic devices, I'm convinced that the use of smart phones and the Internet access they provide (including social media) are among the greatest weapons in Satan's arsenal. Together, they provide a myriad of opportunities to *distract, deceive, and dumb down*. People now live in a cyber world where they create their own reality and unwittingly leave themselves vulnerable to every imaginable form of deception. But we have no reason to surrender. We have the "divinely powerful" weapons of the Spirit and his Word that are at our disposal for the "destruction of fortresses ... destroying speculations and every lofty thing raised up against the knowledge of God" (2 Cor. 10:4-5).

In contrast to the contemporary modes of evangelism and preaching, we see something very different in Scripture. Because man's unbelief is a consequence of the fall and not his environment, entertainment preaching that bypasses the *mind* and appeals to the *emotions* is both dangerous and unbiblical. Without there being a true intellectual understanding of guilt and condemnation before a holy God, genuine repentance cannot occur. For example, unbelievers must grasp the reality of the true gospel, where an explanation of the "wrath of God" precedes one concerning "the love of God"—the reverse of what is typically preached. My point is simply this: sinful people must first *hear* these truths in order to *believe* them and come to a place of genuine *repentance* and *faith* in Christ (Rom. 10:17). As John MacArthur stated:

> *S*alvation is for people who hate their sin. It is for individuals who understand that they have lived in rebellion against a holy God. It is for those who want to turn around to live for God's glory.... Evangelism must take the sinner and measure him against the perfect law of God so that he can see his deficiency[37]

Consistently throughout the New Testament, we witness the Holy Spirit using his Word to penetrate the *mind* in order for sinners and saints to comprehend the Scriptures and apply truth to their lives. This was at the heart of Paul's prayer for the saints that they "may be able to comprehend with all the saints what is the breadth and length and height and depth, and to know the love of Christ which surpasses knowledge, that [they] may be filled up to all the fullness of God" (Eph. 3:18-19).

The *mind* is the key to spiritual growth, which makes Bible exposition so crucial. Expository preaching depends solely upon the Spirit to bring truth to bear upon an individual's conscience, which possesses an instinctive awareness of God's law and warns him concerning his violation of it (Rom. 2:14-16). It addresses "every man's conscience in the sight of God" (2 Cor. 4:2) and brings a man face-to-face with undeniable doctrinal certainties that will either harden or soften his heart (Isa. 55:11).

The great British expositor Martyn Lloyd-Jones diagnosed this danger well:

> *Present-day religion far too often soothes the conscience instead of awakening it; and produces a sense of self-satisfaction and eternal safety rather than a sense of unworthiness and the likelihood of eternal damnation.... There is something even worse than that about the situation as I see it, and that is that present-day preaching does not even annoy men, but leaves them precisely where they were, without a ruffle and without the slightest disturbance.... The church is regarded as a sort of dispensary where drugs and soothing mixtures are distributed and in which everyone should be eased and comforted. And the one theme of the church must be "the love of God". Anyone who happens to break these rules and who produces a disturbing effect upon members of his congregation is regarded as an objectionable person.[38]*

To be sure, this kind of doctrinal preaching is rare in contemporary evangelicalism that has grown accustomed to entertainment preaching and PowerPoint superficiality. Nonetheless, since this was the method exemplified in the Bible

(Neh. 8:8; Acts 7:2-53; 8:27-35; 20:26-27; Luke 4:16-22; 24:27, 32, 44-47), and since we have a divine mandate to "preach the Word" (2 Tim. 4:2), I believe this is the God-ordained method to which pastors must be committed. Peter captures this in his exhortation, "Whoever speaks, *is to do so* as one who is speaking the utterances of God" (1 Peter 4:11).

Furthermore, this is consistent with Paul's emphasis on the *mind* as the primary path to spiritual growth. We see this in his exhortation to the saints in Rome, and by extension, to all of us today. There, he speaks directly to the priority of offering ourselves to God as "a living and holy sacrifice" (Rom. 12:1) by warning us of two important ongoing imperatives: "Do not be conformed to this world, but be transformed by the renewing of your mind, so that you may prove what the will of God is, that which is good and acceptable and perfect" (Rom. 12:2).

The verb "be conformed" translates the Greek verb *sunschematizo*, meaning, "to assume a certain form."[39] It portrays a masquerade, playing a role, or putting on an act according to a script. In this context it refers to assuming an outward expression or form that does not come from within, nor does it reflect an inward reality. Paul is saying, "Don't allow yourself to become something on the outside that you are not on the inside." The prefixed preposition *sun* adds to the meaning of the verb the idea of assuming an expression or form that is patterned after something, in this case, "the world" (*aion*), which G.C. Trench describes as,

> *that floating mass of thoughts, opinions, maxims,*
> *speculations, hopes, impulses, aims, aspirations, at any time*
> *current in the world, which it may be impossible to seize*
> *and accurately define, but which constitute a most real and*
> *effective power, being the moral, or immoral atmosphere*
> *which at every moment of our lives we inhale, again*
> *inevitable to exhale.*[40]

In contrast to allowing ourselves to be "conformed to this world," Paul exhorts believers to "be transformed by the renewing of your mind." The term "transformed" translates the Greek *metamorphousthe*, (lit., "be continually being transformed"), from which we get our English word metamorphosis, which means, "to remodel" or "to change into another form."[41] In this context, it connotes *change in outward appearance that reflects an inner nature*, like a caterpillar becoming a butterfly.

Matthew used this word to describe Jesus' transfiguration: "He was transfigured before them; and His face shone like the sun, and His garments became as white as light" (Matt. 17:2). The effulgence of Christ's glorified inner nature was suddenly manifested—a magnificent illustration of how our inner redeemed nature is to be manifested in our lives to whatever degree possible, a supernatural materialization that will ultimately characterize our glorified state.

Moreover, since Paul's imperative is in the passive voice, we can better understand the profound benefit of his admonition. He is saying we must allow ourselves to undergo a radical and thorough change, one in which *we become on the outside who we really are on the inside.* Our outward conduct must reflect our redeemed inner nature that will one day shine forth like the ineffable glory of Christ to whom we have been forever united. And how does this happen? *"By the renewing of your mind."* The term "renewing" (*anakainosei*) means to cause something to become new and different, with the implication of becoming superior.

So in this context, Paul is making a stark contrast with these two verbs. He is warning against an *outward conformity* to the world *brought about by the world itself* that *does not* accurately reflect the new nature, versus a continual *inner transformation brought about by the renewing of the mind* that *does* accurately reflect the new nature. To paraphrase the meaning, Paul is saying, "Don't let the world shape you into its image and cause you to be who you are not, but rather, through the power of the Spirit and his truth, let the continual renewing of your mind cause you to manifest who you really are, a new creature in Christ, clothed in his righteousness."

THE SPIRIT'S EMPOWERING WORK THROUGH HIS WORD

Obviously, weak, non-doctrinal preaching that merely appeals to the emotions cannot accomplish any of this. Such an inner metamorphosis is the result of an ongoing renewal of the mind empowered by the Holy Spirit and the sanctifying power of his Word. He is the *agent* of regeneration and sanctification, and his Word is his supernatural *instrument*. He is the One who animates an *outward manifestation of holiness* through an *inward transformation of our mind*. This is the work of sanctification—a consequence of a radically different way of thinking, a whole new attitude and disposition (2 Cor. 5:17). Bottom line: *real and lasting life transformation simply cannot occur apart from a continual renewing of the mind.*

Paul reiterates this magnificent truth in 2 Corinthians 3:18: "But we all, with unveiled face, beholding as in a mirror the glory of the Lord, are being transformed into the same image from glory to glory, just as from the Lord, the Spirit." This speaks of the Spirit's internal work of progressive sanctification. It is the Spirit who illuminates the minds of believers so we can understand Scripture when it is heard or read (1 Cor. 2:13-16; Ps. 119:130; Eph. 1:18-19; 1 John 2:27). Through this, we are able to see the glory of God manifested in the face of Christ and become more transformed into his likeness. The Spirit's work of illumination works in concert with those who labor in serious Bible study (2 Tim. 2:15) and with gifted men who have been called to teach his Word (Eph. 4:11-12; 2 Tim. 4:2).

Without question, the mind is crucial in the work of sanctification. It cannot be bypassed. It must be the primary target of every preacher. We are even commanded to "set [our] mind on the things above, not on the things that are on earth" (Col. 3:2). We do this by meditating on the Word of God that produces the *mind of God* within us (Ps. 119). We are to meditate upon his person (Ps. 27:4; 63:6), his Word (Josh. 1:8; Ps 1:2), and his works (Ps. 143:5; 145:5).

But because of our sinful nature, our minds tend to focus on the temporal and ephemeral. We are naturally attracted to the temptations of the world, like a moth to a flame. It is, therefore, the grave responsibility of the preacher to unleash the Word upon his flock and let it do what it alone can do through the agency of the Spirit. Through careful expositions of biblical texts, the Spirit alters the natural gaze of the flesh and causes people to *not* "look . . . at the things which are seen, but at the things which are not seen; for the things which are seen are temporal, but the things which are not seen are eternal"

(2 Cor. 4:16). *This cannot happen apart from doctrinal preaching that focuses primarily on the character of God and his glorious plan of redemption!*

As preachers, we must understand that it is theological *propositions* that define Christianity—*not experience*. Only when we know the Word of God can we "prove what the will of God is, that which is good and acceptable and perfect" (Rom. 12:2). And when his will becomes our will, our "living and holy sacrifice" is "pleasing to Him" because it is an expression of his nature that has now become ours through the miracle of regeneration. Only then can we "be salt and light (Matt. 5:13–14), purifying and enlightening contemporary culture."[42]

Paul wants us to understand these basic spiritual truths because they are foundational to our sanctification and ministry. We cannot present ourselves as a "living and holy sacrifice" that is "acceptable to God" if we allow ourselves to "be conformed to this world." Moreover, no true believer will refuse to allow the Holy Spirit to renew his or her mind. Those who are according to the Spirit set their minds on the things of the Spirit. It is natural to them, just as natural as it is for those who are according to the flesh to set their minds on the things of the flesh (Rom. 8:5-8, 12-14).

Paul complained of professing Christians who were really enemies of the cross of Christ because they set their minds on earthly things (Phil. 3:18,19). The flesh will war against the Spirit, but it cannot overcome it because it is God who is at work in us, both to will and to work for his good pleasure. It is because the true believer desires to do the will of God that he will have a hunger for the Word of God. The reason the true Christian loves the Bible above every other book in the world is because it is the pure milk of the Word. This is what true believers long for the most. Nowhere else can they find what the mind and will of God is for their lives. Unless people first have a Spirit-produced desire to do the will of God, they will never saturate their minds with the Word of God. They read and study their Bibles to know it, not as scholars or theologians, but as Christians—to live it, not critique or dispute it.

Paul spoke of this often. As stated earlier, he told the Colossians, "We proclaim Him, admonishing every man and teaching every man with all wisdom, that we may present every man complete in Christ" (Col. 1:28), and again in 3:16, "Let the word of Christ richly dwell within you, with all wisdom, teaching and admonishing one another with psalms and hymns and spiritual songs, singing with thankfulness in your hearts to God." Here we see there are both a *moral* and an *intellectual* component to this transformation (this continual process of renewal).

Similarly, Jesus prayed to the Father: "Sanctify them in the truth; Your word is truth" (John 17:17). This requires an intellectual understanding of propositional truth. Under the inspiration of the Spirit, Peter communicated the same thing when he said:

> *Therefore, prepare your minds for action, keep*
> *sober in spirit, fix your hope completely on the*
> *grace to be brought to you at the revelation of Jesus*
> *Christ. As obedient children, do not be conformed*
> *to the former lusts which were yours in your*
> *ignorance, but like the Holy One who called you, be*
> *holy yourselves also in all your behavior; because it*
> *is written, "You shall be holy, for I am holy."*
>
> *(1 Peter 1:13-16)*

Once again, the mind cannot be continually renewed apart from the faithful exposition of the truth. This is the preacher's great responsibility. Since no one automatically drifts toward holiness, we must decisively commit ourselves to it by submitting to the Holy Spirit on a moment-by-moment basis as he reveals himself to us through his Word (Gal. 5:16). This is why doctrinal, expositional preaching is so crucial.

PAUL'S CONFIDENCE IN EXPOSITIONAL PREACHING

Paul was a preacher of "the Word of God" (*ho logos tou theou*); a phrase used over forty times in the New Testament. Obviously, Jesus preached it as well (Luke 5:1), along with the apostles (Acts 4:31; 6:2). It was the revelation of God transmitted to the prophets and apostles through God's Spirit.

Because "all Scripture is inspired by God and profitable for teaching, for reproof, for correction, for training in righteousness" (2 Tim. 3:16), every New Testament preacher proclaimed it with careful precision to ensure it was delivered in the same way it was originally received (2 Cor. 2:17; 4:2). Paul acknowledged that he had received "a revelation of Jesus Christ" (Gal. 1:12), therefore, given the supernatural source of the truth revealed, he admonished Timothy to "be diligent to present yourself approved to God as a workman who does not need to be ashamed, accurately handling the word of truth" (2 Tim. 2:15).

Unfortunately, this warning has gone unheeded in the ranks of evangelicalism, allowing the thriving bacteria of error to become septic in the church. The fetid stench of hypocrisy now pollutes the very air we breathe. Many evangelicals cannot even agree on the definition of "Christian," which logically confuses the very definition of "the church of the living God, the pillar and support of the truth" (1 Tim. 3:15). When a mere profession of faith without the accompanying validation of a changed life can define a "Christian," the church becomes the most dangerous place on earth, an incubation chamber for false professions and a dead faith that does not lead to salvation. Expository preaching is the only God-ordained declarative genre that can guard against this.

Given the never-ending threat of compromise and satanic deception, pastors must be all the more committed to this kind of preaching. This is why we are to "devote ourselves to prayer and to the ministry of the word" (Acts 6:4). As stated before, the apostle Paul understood this. We see this in his testimony where he says, "Of this church I was made a minister according to the stewardship from God bestowed on me for your benefit, so that I might fully carry out the preaching of the word of God" (Col. 1:25). He later expanded upon this conviction saying,

> We proclaim Him, admonishing every man and
> teaching every man with all wisdom, so that we
> may present every man complete in Christ. For
> this purpose also I labor, striving according to
> His power, which mightily works within me.
>
> (Col. 3:28-29)

The primary emphasis of Paul's ministry is summarized in three verbs: *proclaim, admonish,* and *teach.* How clear and simple! This is God's method for building his church, for growing his redeemed into maturity and the likeness of Christ.

Paul's *proclamation* included preaching, but also extended beyond it to involve any form of public declaration as the term *katangello* ("proclaim") implied. But it also incorporated both "admonishing" and "teaching," which are essentially synonyms meaning "instruct."

"Admonishing" (*noutheteo*) carries the idea of warning, exhorting, encouraging, or correcting, which was one of the primary aspects of Paul's ministry. For example, in Acts 20:31 we learn how passionate he was to this end: "Night and day for a period of three years I did not cease to admonish each one with tears." He also exhorted the Colossians saying, "Let the word of Christ richly dwell within you, with all wisdom teaching and admonishing one another" (Col. 3:16; cf. 2 Thess. 3:14-15; Rom. 15:14).

Similarly, "teaching" (*didasko*) carries many of the same implications, but with the added emphasis of imparting practical doctrinal truth "with all wisdom, so that we may present every man complete in Christ" (Col. 3:28). While both *admonishing* and *teaching* are the responsibility of every believer and are at the very heart of the Great Commission (Matt. 28:20), it is the primary task of faithful pastors. An overseer must be able to "[hold] fast the faithful word which is in accordance with the teaching, that he may be able both to exhort in sound doctrine and refute those who contradict" (Titus 1:9; cf. 1 Tim. 3:2). This is inherent in Paul's clear call to expository preaching recorded in 1 Timothy 4:13 where he writes to Timothy, "Until I come, give attention to the public reading of Scripture, to exhortation and teaching." We are to *read, explain,* and *apply* the Word of God. Because this is so important, he went on to exhort the young pastor to "pay close attention to yourself and to your teaching; persevere in these things" (v. 16).

Paul was confident in this one method, which I prefer to summarize under the heading of expository preaching. He was devoted to *proclaiming, admonishing,* and *teaching.* As pastors, we must do the same. This is far more than just covering material, or disseminating theological facts, or facilitating discussions. It is far more than wandering around a stage sharing random thoughts and cutting up with an audience. We have the solemn responsibility to know the Word and make it come alive in the minds of our listeners so it will take root in their hearts and produce much fruit for the glory of God.

OTHER EXAMPLES OF EXPOSITIONAL PREACHERS IN SCRIPTURE

The spirit of expository preaching as the primary means by which the flock is spiritually fed and nourished can be seen in the Old Testament account of revival that occurred among the Jewish remnant that returned to Jerusalem after seventy years of Babylonian captivity, under the leadership of Nehemiah. What is really fascinating is how God brought about revival through the exposition of his Word by a scribe named Ezra, a man who "had set his heart to study the law of the Lord and to practice *it,* and to teach *His* statutes and ordinances in Israel" (Ezra 7:10). Nehemiah describes at least a six-hour sermon where all the people stood for Ezra's exposition as he, "read from the book, from the law of God, translating to give the sense so that they understood the reading" (Neh. 8:8).

While some of the remnant spoke Aramaic during their exile and may have needed help with translation, the idea conveyed in the phrase "translating to give the sense so that they understood the reading" (v. 8) carries the idea of *exposition.* The word, "translating" (from the Hebrew root *pārāš*), means *to make distinct, declare.*[43] Ezra literally explained or exposited the meaning of God's Word so the people could understand it. The response was to be expected, "for all the people were weeping when they heard the words of the law" (v. 9). Herein is the power of the Word. As doctrinal preachers we must follow Ezra's example.

We must also emulate Jesus, who spoke to the confused men on the road to Emmaus: "And beginning with Moses and with all the prophets, He explained to them the things concerning Himself in all the Scriptures" (Luke 24:27). Once again, the response is typical. They reflected on what had just happened and said to one another, "Were not our hearts burning within us while He was speaking to us on the road, while He was explaining the Scriptures to us?" In similar fashion, when Jesus later appeared to his disciples after his resurrection, he "opened their minds to understand the Scriptures" (Luke 24:45). Armed with truth and later empowered by the indwelling Spirit, they set the world on fire for Christ.

Throughout the New Testament we see many examples of expository preaching. Consider Jesus' sermon in the synagogue

(Luke 4:16-22), the sermons of Peter (Acts 2:14-36), Stephen (Acts 7:2-53), Philip (Acts 8:31-35), Paul (Acts 17:16-31), and James (Acts 15:14-21). In fact, the New Testament epistles were essentially written expositions. When this kind of expositional preaching is missing from evangelical pulpits, the church is weakened and Christ is dishonored.

THE BARREN TREE PRODUCED BY NON-DOCTRINAL PREACHING

It has been my experience on countless occasions to witness the transforming power of doctrinal preaching in my life, and in the lives of those to whom I have the honor of preaching. But I have also seen the sorrowful results of weak gospel presentations and insipid, devotional, non-doctrinal, man-centered preaching that is more concerned with reconciling *man to man* than *man to God*. Weak pulpits inevitably produce weak Christians who will show little resemblance to Christ and bear little fruit for his glory.

A steady diet of anecdotes, humor, and rambling comments based upon some Bible verse or Bible story is tantamount to eating junk food lacking in nutrition. Unfortunately, like the "junk-food-aholic," undernourished Christians lose their awe of God and cannot say with David, "On the glorious splendor of Your majesty, and on Your wonderful works, I will meditate" (Ps. 145:5). Just strike up a friendly conversation with people from these kinds of churches and see where it goes. Seldom, if ever, will you detect an insatiable appetite for the Word, a joyful commitment to holiness, a burden for the lost, or a thirst for the soul-satisfying presence of God within their soul. From their perspective, they have all of Christ they need and want. Better yet, ask them what they read, as I have sometimes asked. If they read at all, their bibliography will typically revolve around the best-selling books in the Christian bookstore, most of which contain serious theological error.

How tragic! It should be no surprise that in churches where true expository preaching does not exist, biblical discernment is equally non-existent. Just look at the evidence. Churches by the thousands fall victim to religious fads that come and go like hit songs on the radio. Remember the ecumenical *Promise Keepers* movement in the 1990s that fed hungry men a liberal gospel seasoned with charismatic error from a smorgasbord that seemingly had a deliberate disregard for biblical principles of sanctification essential for spiritual growth in men. Ten years later in the year 2000, a new fad captured the attention of the church. Like preteen groupies slobbering over a teenage boy band, undiscerning evangelicals ran wildly after the *Prayer of Jabez* that peddled a spiritual elixir guaranteed to elevate us to a higher level of Christianity. By the hundreds of thousands, professing believers guzzled its perverted understanding of prayer, prosperity, and the providence of God. A few years later the *Purpose Driven Life* swept the world with its quasi-evangelical content, promoting a non-offensive gospel that continues to attract individuals who, in many instances, may have no understanding of the true gospel of God yet are convinced they are heaven bound.

Meanwhile, naïve yet hungry evangelicals clamored all the more for the next spiritual fantasy, and Satan delivered with a fictional novel entitled *The Shack* that attempted to answer the question, "Why does God allow evil?" Despite its blasphemous misrepresentations of the Trinity that violated God's second commandment prohibiting the worship of man-made representations of himself (Ex. 20:4-6), the evangelical response was nothing short of euphoric. Despite its trivialization of the holiness of God and its persistent assaults on orthodox Christianity, it was so popular it was made into a movie.

Then came the next shooting star flashing across the evangelical sky, the truth-hating *Emergent Church* phenomena where avant-garde evangelicals congregate in candlelit rooms with a glass of Chardonnay to pool their ignorance and proudly bash those who love the truth.

The point is this: *doctrinal preaching protects against these dangers. As we have seen, Paul was confident with one method: expositional preaching.* Believers are to be "constantly nourished on the words of the faith and . . . sound doctrine" (1 Tim. 4:6).

Whenever we see God high and lifted up in his Word, we are "laid bare to the eyes of Him with whom we have to do" (Heb. 4:13) and experience a mixture of sheer terror in confession and utter joy in forgiveness. We become like Isaiah when he was exposed by the white light of divine holiness and cried out, "Woe is me, for I am ruined!" (Isa. 6:5).

This is the kind of exposure the church needs.

WHAT EXPOSITORY PREACHING IS NOT

Too often, what passes for expository preaching is little more than a brief commentary on a passage that serves as a launching pad for a preacher's random thoughts, human opinions, and incoherent meanderings—and with no clear theme, unity, or direction. Worse yet, many times the so-called "exposition" has nothing to do with God's intended meaning.

Early in my ministry I was struck by ten suggestions of what expository preaching is *not*, derived from Faris D. Whitesell's book, *Power in Expository Preaching*. Perhaps it will be helpful to you. Here's his list:

1. It is not a commentary running from word to word and verse to verse without unity, outline, and pervasive drive.

2. It is not rambling comments and offhand remarks about a passage without a background of thorough exegesis and logical order.

3. It is not a mass of disconnected suggestions and inferences based on the surface meaning of a passage but not sustained by a depth-and-breadth study of the text.

4. It is not pure exegesis, no matter how scholarly, if it lacks a theme, thesis, outline, and development.

5. It is not a mere structural outline of a passage with a few supporting comments but without other rhetorical and sermonic elements.

6. It is not a topical homily using scattered parts of the passage but omitting discussion of other equally important parts.

7. It is not a chopped-up collection of grammatical findings and quotations from commentaries without a fusing of these elements into a smooth, flowing, interesting, and compelling message.

8. It is not a Sunday-school-lesson type of discussion that has an outline of the contents, informality, and fervency but lacks sermonic structure and rhetorical ingredients.

9. It is not a Bible reading that links a number of scattered passages treating a common theme but fails to handle any of them in a thorough, grammatical, and contextual manner.

10. It is not the ordinary devotional or prayer-meeting talk that combines running commentary, rambling remarks, disconnected suggestions, and personal reactions into a semi-inspirational discussion but lacks the benefit of the basic exegetical-contextual study and persuasive elements.[44]

THE BENEFITS AND BLESSINGS OF EXPOSITORY PREACHING

With this in mind, it is important to encourage Bible expositors with some of the wonderful benefits and blessings that I have personally discovered as a Bible expositor. I am sure there are other examples, and perhaps some of my observations may overlap others, but I hope they will be both helpful and encouraging.

1. Expository preaching reflects the conviction that the Bible is the inspired, inerrant, infallible, authoritative, all-sufficient Word of God.

2. Expository preaching accurately expounds the principles and doctrines of a text consistent with the author's original intent.

3. Expository preaching explains the God-intended meaning of a text in a manner consistent with the normal use of language and in its original context.

4. Expository preaching provides the only legitimate source of authority for the preacher.

5. Expository preaching facilitates the declaration of the whole counsel of God.

6. Expository preaching eliminates the danger of "hobbyhorse" preaching and the curse of being a "one-string banjo."

7. Expository preaching forces the preacher to interpret difficult and controversial passages.

8. Expository preaching guards against the infiltration of worldly philosophies and human opinions.

9. Expository preaching imitates the preaching of Christ and the apostles.

10. Expository preaching protects against misinterpretation and misapplication.

11. Expository preaching models the proper way to study and apply Scripture.

12. Expository preaching demonstrates the unity and perspicuity of Scripture.

13. Expository preaching calls attention to other parallel passages in Scripture.

14. Expository preaching demonstrates *how*, *why*, and *where* every passage fits into Scripture as a whole.

15. Expository preaching synthesizes Bible doctrines and develops a systematic theology.

16. Expository preaching taps into the infinite reservoir of divine revelation.

17. Expository preaching demonstrates the timeless and contemporary practicality of God's Word.

18. Expository preaching causes a congregation to grow in the grace and knowledge of God and develop spiritual unity, maturity, and discernment.

19. Expository preaching builds a library of biblical interpretation that can be accessed for future reference.

20. Expository preaching develops the preacher as a trustworthy steward of the mysteries of God.

21. Expository preaching forces the preacher to stay focused on the Word, resulting in his own spiritual nourishment, growth, and power.

22. Expository preaching insures that a preacher's topic arises out of Scripture directly and not from himself.

23. Expository preaching creates an insatiable appetite for the Word of God in both the preacher and his congregation.

24. Expository preaching motivates a preacher to live in a spirit of prayer and communion with God so he can rightly divide the Word of truth and proclaim it with authority, boldness, and love.

25. Expository preaching causes a preacher to stay lost in the sheer wonder of divine revelation and the pure grace of his most solemn calling.

A FINAL WORD

It is beyond the scope of our discussion to specify the actual steps and process of expository preaching. Others have already done this in great detail and far better than I could ever hope to do. I have greatly benefited from the excellent book written by John MacArthur, Jr., and the faculty of the Master's Seminary entitled *Rediscovering Expository Preaching: Balancing the Science and Art of Biblical Exposition.*[45] I would also recommend D. Martyn Lloyd-Jones' *Preaching and Preachers,*[46] along with Charles Spurgeon's *Lectures to My Students.*[47] But in addition to these sources, one of the best ways to understand the art and science of expository preaching is to listen to great expositors.

As we have seen thus far in this book, Paul was *consumed with God's glory,* the foundational key principle for effective ministry. Therefore he was *content with his suffering, convinced of his calling, controlled by one message,* and *confident with one method: expository preaching.* For this reason, he could say with utmost sincerity, "And we proclaim Him, admonishing every man and teaching every man with all wisdom" (Col. 1:28). These principles were all pillars of his ministry, along with two more that emerge out of Colossians 1:24-29, namely, *he was committed to one end*—the subject of the next chapter—and *confirmed by one power,* the subject of the final chapter. It is my sincere prayer that every man who has been called into this highest of all callings will share these convictions.

HOLY BIBLE, BOOK DIVINE

Holy Bible, book divine,
Precious treasure, thou art mine;
Mine to tell me whence I came;
Mine to teach me what I am.

Mine to chide me when I rove;
Mine to show a Savior's love;
Mine thou art to guide and guard;
Mine to punish or reward.

Mine to comfort in distress;
Suff'ring in this wilderness;
Mine to show, by living faith,
Man can triumph over death.

Mine to tell of joys to come,
And the rebel sinner's doom:
O thou Holy Book divine,
Precious treasure, thou are mine. Amen.

John Burton (1773–1822)

CHAPTER 6

KEY PRINCIPLE SIX:
COMMITTED TO ONE END

"... that we may present every man complete in Christ."

Colossians 1:28

Next to my burden for the lost, my greatest sorrow in ministry is the lack of adoration for the majesty and holiness of God among professing evangelicals. While this is largely a consequence of the powerful temptations of a satanic world system bent on providing limitless and seemingly irresistible opportunities for idolatry and self-worship, it is also rooted in a shallow understanding of the perfections of God's character and a lack of desire to know him, especially in prayer. There is little fear of God these days—little trembling in holiness. Not many mourn over their sin, though many secretly delight in it.

Many Christians are content to live in the swamps of earthly pleasures rather than the highlands of heavenly promises, preferring to fix their eyes on what is seen that is temporary, rather than on what is unseen that is eternal (2 Cor. 4:18). Just look at where Christians spend their money. Very little is invested in the kingdom. Few lay up their treasures in heaven (Matt. 6:19-20), which betrays the idolatry of their hearts, for, as Jesus says, "Where your treasure is, there your heart will be also" (Matt. 6:21). It is impossible for people who are willingly biblically illiterate to love Christ. You cannot love whom you do not know, and whom you love, you want to know more and better. The Jesus they love will be the Jesus of their own imagination. They love him because they invented him.

Encountering mature saints who manifest the opposite of all this provides a stark contrast to the kind of apathetic irreverence that is so grievous to faithful pastors. Is it not wonderful to interact with some brother or sister in Christ who, with full-throated praise, can say with David:

> I will bless the Lord at all times; His praise shall
> continually be in my mouth. My soul will make
> its boast in the Lord; the humble will hear it and
> rejoice. O magnify the Lord with me; and let us
> exalt His name together.
>
> (Ps. 34:1-3)

But saints who embody this kind of life-worship and truly enjoy the unsearchable riches of Christ are few and far between these days. It is little wonder, therefore, that so few experience the soul-satisfying joy of God's presence deep within their soul that would cause them to humbly bow in adoration and say with the prophet: "The Lord is in His holy temple. Let all the earth be silent before Him" (Hab. 2:20).

Nothing is transcendent anymore. I am not even sure most Christians understand what the word "transcendent" means in the context of corporate worship. Just look at the ultra-casual and even immodest attire people wear to church these days. One church sign I read recently makes my point. It said: "Our pastor wears jeans so you can too!" Talk about misplaced priorities! But everything in our postmodern culture is casual, ordinary, and unremarkable these days, even among believers—as if we have forgotten that we "have been bought with a price: therefore glorify God in your body" (1 Cor. 6:20).

There even seems to be an unconscious desperation to erase any line of distinction between the church and the world, and between Christians and non-Christians. Far too many believers seem to live a ho-hum Christian life in an unrewarding world, and then transport their earthbound reality onto a God who is *totally other*—a God who is inexpressibly glorious, infinitely holy, and exhilarating beyond imagination. But they do not see it. Nothing seems to evoke the kind of awe that would cause David to say, "On the glorious splendor of Your majesty and on Your wonderful works, I will meditate. Men shall speak of the power of Your awesome acts, and I will tell of Your greatness" (Ps. 145:5-6). In fact, today, because everything is considered "awesome" no matter how trivial, nothing is truly awesome—except the thrice-Holy God of the universe. But few see it, and among those who may be somewhat aware, few seem to care.

I grieve knowing that even among professing believers in doctrinally sound churches, few habitually come into the presence of God in private worship. In fact, in some circles, personal piety is considered legalistic, an affront to grace. Sadly there are far too few who know the breathless wonder of communing with the living God. The general apathy toward prayer meetings is a testimony to this. Few seem to care about really knowing God. Oh, they want his blessings, but they do not really want *him*. It is the corrupt and selfish love of a harlot that loves the money and gifts better than the one who gives them. Christ will not be loved in this way. The bride of Christ must love him for himself, not just for what he gives. This was

Satan's accusation against Job. For many, even Bible study is motivated more out of a desire to know the *Word of God* than a yearning to know the *God of the Word*; or to be the star of the Sunday school class rather than to enjoy an intimate fellowship with the Lover of their soul.

In light of this, it has been my observation, primarily in our affluent society, that many Christians have no real longing for heaven. I fear many would not even be disappointed if they were told (falsely) that God would not be there! Most people's thoughts of heaven are no better than the Muslim's paradise. The thought of being reunited with departed loved ones is far more appealing to most than the promise of unrestricted personal fellowship with the Triune God that caused Paul to say, "We exult in hope of the glory of God" (Rom. 5:2; cf. 1 John 3:2).

THE PATH TO MATURITY

Given this pervasive irreverence, the question before us is quite simple: What needs to be done? And the answer lies, at least in part, in Paul's testimony in Colossians 1:28: "We proclaim Him, admonishing every man and teaching every man with all wisdom, so that we may present every man complete in Christ." Our people must be awakened and taught who God is, and the blessings that belong to those who are reconciled to him through faith in Christ and who walk in his likeness.

Paul was *committed to this one end*. As we have examined in the previous chapter, the primary activities of his ministry can be summarized in three verbs: *proclaim, admonish,* and *teach.* But what was the goal? The answer: "So that we may present every man complete in Christ" (v. 28).

"Complete" (Greek: *teleios*), can also be translated "mature," or "perfect." The term was used to denote the quality of sacrificial animals that must be without blemish, such as the Passover lamb in Exodus 12:5. We also see this in the characterization of Noah, who was described as "a righteous man, blameless in his time; Noah walked with God" (Gen. 6:9). The Greeks held in high esteem one who, through instruction, had developed a subject or craft to a point where he was considered the "perfect man," one who had reached a place of "maturity" or "completeness." It is likely that Paul's inspired use of this term would have been understood in that cultural context, consistent with his other usage of the term (1 Cor. 2:6; 14:20; Phil. 3:15; Col. 4:12; cf. Matt. 5:48; 19:21).[48]

Paul was passionate to "present every man complete in Christ," that is, to help every believer become more like Christ. He also understood the pathway to spiritual maturity was allowing the Word of God to dwell in them richly (Col. 3:16). Because the Holy Spirit works through the Word, he knew this was his responsibility to those he had led to Christ and those he shepherded. With the phrase, "present every man," he employs sacerdotal language of sacrifice, as though he were a priest offering up sacrifices to God that were "complete," "mature," or "perfect;" referring to spiritually mature, Christlike believers. This was the burden of his heart. This is what drove him.

Obviously, every pastor should follow this example. This was what animated Epaphras' fervency in prayer for his fellow saints in Colossae—Paul describing him as "a bondslave of Jesus Christ . . . always laboring earnestly for you in his prayers, that you may stand perfect and fully assured in all the will of God" (Col. 4:12).

He knew that mere preaching was simply not enough. Following Jesus' example, he understood how personal discipleship was also essential in the process of imparting and applying truth to individual lives—and what a wonderful thing to behold. Every faithful pastor can agree with John who said, "I have no greater joy than this, to hear of my children walking in the truth" (3 John 4).

THE PROBLEM OF SPIRITUAL IMMATURITY

Spiritual immaturity has been and always will be a problem in the church. Instead of becoming more like Christ, many remain in a state of spiritual infancy, and blissfully so. Someone may boast, for example, of having been a Christian for thirty years, when, in reality, he has only been a Christian one year, thirty times. Very little change has taken place over the course of such a person's life. But faithful preaching and shepherding will address this, and by God's grace, bring about real, measurable, and enduring change.

Based upon Paul's ministry, combined with the statements he made in Colossians 1:28-29 and 2:2 (which we will examine more closely), we see at least three categories of shepherding priorities that must be implemented if we ever hope to see people grow up into spiritual adulthood that truly honors and reflects Christ.

1. We must *proclaim* the exalted character of God.

2. We must *admonish* others concerning the severity and scope of idolatry in their hearts.

3. We must *teach* others the importance of intimacy with God that leads to maturity.

Hopefully these guiding principles can serve us well as pastors in our quest to "present every man complete in Christ."

SHEPHERDING PRIORITY NUMBER ONE:
WE MUST PROCLAIM THE EXALTED CHARACTER OF GOD.

We must help our people see how the attributes of God are being manifested, accomplishing all that he has decreed in eternity past to bring glory to himself. They must understand that the *perfections*[49] of his character are eternally, infinitely, and completely active in his essence at all times, not only in the passage under examination, but also in their lives today. With Peter we must "proclaim the excellencies of Him who has called you out of darkness into His marvelous light" (1 Peter 2:9).

While addressing young men who were potential candidates for ministry, the eighteenth-century New England Puritan preacher, Cotton Mather, said this:

> *The office of Christian ministry, rightly understood, is the most honourable, and important, that any man in the whole world can ever sustain; and it will be one of the wonders and employments of eternity to consider the reasons why the wisdom and goodness of God assigned this to imperfect and guilty man! . . . The great design and intention of the office of a Christian preacher are to restore the throne and dominion of God in the souls of men; to display in the most lively colours, and proclaim in the clearest language, the wonderful perfections, offices and grace of the Son of God; and to attract the souls of men into a*

state of everlasting friendship with him.[50]

This is our calling as pastors, and we do it because we love Christ and are committed to one end: "presenting every man complete" in him. And this starts by addressing the issue of who God *really* is, not who he has been made out to be. This, as I stated earlier, is the reason why so many believers lack the appropriate adoration for the majesty and holiness of God.

For most evangelicals, God is simply too small. They do not see him as he really is, as he has revealed himself in creation and Scripture. The inspiring words of the psalmist in Psalm 19 concerning the overwhelming works of God (natural revelation) and the sixfold description of the transforming Word of God (special revelation) should cause us all to shout, "Let the words of my mouth and the meditation of my heart, be acceptable in Your sight, O Lord, my rock and my Redeemer" (v. 14). But sadly, these overpowering realities make little difference in those surfeited with the materialistic pleasures of this world.

Worse yet, instead of God being the self-existent, uncreated Creator, Sustainer, Redeemer, and Consummator of all things, he has been reduced to a god who merely exists to make us happy. Instead of being the omniscient, omnipotent Sovereign who knows the end from the beginning and works all things after the counsel of his will, he has been reduced to a god who merely responds to the will of human beings. Instead of being the ineffable Tetragrammaton to be feared and worshipped, he is just a mysterious, unknowable, uninvolved force indifferent to our plight. Instead of being an infinitely holy God who will judge sin and return in power and great glory, he has been redefined as a smiley-faced god who winks at sin and has no further purposes concerning people on earth. Rather than Christ having the preeminence in all things, he is little more than an afterthought if thought of at all, except, of course, on Sundays at church.

The staggering truth of divine immanence alone should drive us all to our faces in solemn worship. To know that our immeasurable God is so intimately involved in his redeemed that he knows our thoughts, ways, and words—that there is nothing in us that is hidden from his sight—should cause us to say with David, "Such knowledge is too wonderful for me;

it is too high, I cannot attain to it" (Ps. 139:6). But our people are typically distracted, even obsessed, with matters that are eternally insignificant. Consequently, adoring the majesty and holiness of God simply gets lost in the cultural fog.

For example, how many believers do you honestly think ever meditate on the doctrine of justification and God's plan of redemption? Very few at best. Most churchgoers are completely indifferent to matters like what version of the doctrine of justification is taught, or the nature and necessity of the new birth, or what view of sanctification is espoused. And for those who do, only a handful will break out in a doxology of praise like Paul and say: "Oh, the depth of the riches both of the wisdom and knowledge of God! How unsearchable are His judgments and unfathomable His ways! . . . For from Him and through Him and to Him are all things. To Him be the glory forever. Amen" (Rom. 11:33, 36). To be sure, this must be the sincere doxology of a pastor's heart. If not, there is something terribly wrong in his life and he must take serious inventory to determine where his heart has wandered away from the path of godliness.

In light of this, every pastor must put the glory of Christ on display in his life, in his preaching, and in his shepherding. This is why God has given the church pastor-teachers—to help the elect of God "attain to the unity of the faith, and of the knowledge of the Son of God, to a mature man, to the measure of the stature which belongs to the fullness of Christ" (Eph. 4:13). And there is no greater message than the gospel to exalt the character of God.

PROCLAIMING THE GLORY OF GOD IN THE ATONEMENT

In his farewell address in John 13, after he had dismissed Judas who was under Satan's full control, Jesus said, "Now is the Son of Man glorified, and God is glorified in Him; if God is glorified in Him, God will also glorify Him in Himself, and will glorify Him immediately" (John 13:31-32).

Here we see the perfections of Christ in the glory of his atonement—a subject worthy of our bold, unfettered proclamation. In the Old Testament, the title "Son of Man" is associated with the *glory* of Christ (as in Daniel 7), but in the Synoptic Gospels it is associated with his *suffering*. And here the Lord uses this title of himself to unite both his *glory* and his *suffering.* Indeed, there is perhaps no greater manifestation of the glory of God than in the atoning work of the Son. We see the Son glorified in his inconceivable *condescension*, in his infinite *mercy*, and in his unassailable *power* as he goes to the cross to render powerless the effects of sin, Satan, and death.

God the Father is also glorified in the Son through his *sovereignty* and *faithfulness* to fulfill his covenant promises to Adam and Eve and their descendants. In the protoevangelium of Genesis 3:15, he promised to provide a redeemer, later pictured in the innocent animal he killed to provide a covering for sin (v. 21). His *sovereignty* and *faithfulness* are also put on display by providing a way of salvation to the elect of Israel and among the Gentiles who have been grafted into the root of Abrahamic blessing—the necessary elements for the dawning messianic kingdom. He is also glorified in his *omniscience* as he carries out a plan of redemption that not only *forgives sinners*, but also *declares them to be righteous* through the *imputed righteousness of his perfect sacrifice.*

We see him glorified in his *holy hatred of sin*, when he poured out his wrath upon his Son to satisfy his perfect justice. We see him glorified in his *omnipotence* that would not only raise Jesus from the dead, but also give spiritual life to dead sinners and one day raise *them* from the dead. We see him glorified in his *love* that is magnified in a way so profound, John said: "In this is love, not that we loved God, but that He loved us and sent his Son to be the propitiation for our sins" (1 John 4:10).

Frankly, every attribute, every perfection of deity, is dramatically displayed on the cross of Calvary. For this reason Jesus says, "If God is glorified in Him, God will also glorify Him in Himself, and will glorify Him immediately" (John 13:32). This speaks of the glory given to the Son as a result of his perfect obedience to the Father's will, his sacrificial death, resurrection, and exaltation to the right hand of the Father in glory. Paul summarized this in Phil. 2:10 when he said: "Therefore also God highly exalted Him, and bestowed on Him the name which is above every name, that at the name of Jesus every knee should bow, of those who are in heaven, and on earth, and under the earth and that every tongue should confess that Jesus Christ is Lord, to the glory of God the Father."

How absolutely thrilling it is to behold the perfections of

Christ in the glory of his atonement. And this is what we must proclaim as pastors. We must help our people fix their gaze upon the glory of the Lord, for this is the means the Spirit uses to transform his redeemed ever more into the likeness of Christ. The godly Puritan theologian John Owen said it best:

> *Let us live in the constant contemplation of the glory of Christ, and virtue will proceed from him to repair all our decays, to renew a right spirit within us, and to cause us to abound in all duties of obedience.... It will fix the soul unto that object which is suited to give it delight, complacency, and satisfaction.... When the mind is filled with thoughts of Christ and his glory, when the soul thereon cleaves unto him with intense affections, they will cast out, or not give admittance unto, those causes of spiritual weakness and indisposition.... And nothing will so much excite and encourage our souls hereunto as a constant view of Christ and his glory.*[51]

SHEPHERDING PRIORITY NUMBER TWO:
WE MUST ADMONISH OTHERS CONCERNING THE SEVERITY AND SCOPE OF IDOLATRY IN THEIR HEART.

If we are truly committed to presenting every man complete in Christ (Col. 1:28), we must not only help our people see the magnificent outworkings of his perfections in their lives, but we must also help them see the subtle ways they distort his character in how they think and live. They must understand how this is more than apathy; more than ignorance; more than even practical atheism—it is *idolatry*!

Whenever someone worships the true God falsely, or redefines him, or attributes to him that which is not true, that person perverts the truth of who God is and lives as though he is not who he says he is. Then, like individuals in ancient Israel, he subjects himself to the judgment of the God *who is*. Our people must hear this warning, lest they place themselves under a cloud of divine chastening that results in their losing their blessing and eternal reward. They must see the hideous nature of idolatry. They must witness our disdain for any distortion of God's perfections or purposes in our life. If this is not evident in a pastor, he is not sent from God. He is no different than the false prophets of Judah of whom the Lord said, "Do not listen to the words of the prophets who are prophesying to you. They are leading you into futility; they speak a vision of their own imagination, not from the mouth of the Lord" (Jer. 23:16-17). Any man who truly loves God—pastor or not—will be zealous for his glory and thus repulsed by any form of idolatry that distracts him from loving and serving the one true God.

When our people see how severe and extensive idolatry is in their hearts, they will more clearly see sin and the world for what they are, as exceedingly sinful and evil, and that to be a friend of the world is to make themselves an enemy of God. They will then be able to better grasp the words of the English Puritan, William Gurnall, who said: "When you, Christian, act unholy, you sin at a high rate indeed. Others sin against the light of God in their consciences. That is the furthest they can go. But you sin against the life of God in your heart."[52]

Unbelievers enslaved by life-dominating sins will often acknowledge a love/hate relationship with the temptations that entice them. They love their sin, but hate its consequences. Therefore, they are constantly trying to find ways to have their sin and avoid its consequences, even to the extent of murdering their own offspring in the womb. The more unnatural a sin is, the more horrid, and the more someone must sin against the natural light of conscience. The same is true of Christians who, though not enslaved, foolishly capitulate to temptation, as we all do. Unbelievers will sin with the full consent of their will, whereas true believers sin against their will. They wish they had done otherwise (Rom. 7:15,16). But especially for the unregenerate who function apart from the restraint of the indwelling Spirit—whether it's alcohol, drugs, sex, gambling, food, work, overspending, or any other alluring pleasure—*seductions will seem irresistible*, even though they know the consequences will be dire.

Scripture often uses the concept of idolatry to illustrate this devastating spiritual phenomenon. God hates idolatry more than any other kind of sin. For this reason, the first two of his ten commandments prohibit worshipping any other gods but him or making any likeness of him (Ex. 20:3-6). It is here the souls of men and women rise or fall. His Law warns that substitute gods will inevitably damn those who worship them. Jeremiah said, "Can a man make gods for himself? Yet they are not gods!" (Jer. 16:20). But it has never stopped people from trying.

Man is by nature a religious being. He is made in God's image to worship him. But because of his sin nature, he "[suppresses] the truth" that is "evident within [him]" through reason and conscience (Rom. 1:18-19). Paul goes on to describe the process and catastrophic consequences of inventing substitute gods (vv. 21-23).

Eventually, God abandons a society and allows it to be enslaved by the gods it has chosen, resulting in unrestrained immorality, a burning desire for homosexuality, and a depraved mind capable of unimaginable evil (vv. 24-32). Scripture is filled with examples of this forbidden worship. Idolatry is described as:

o   Bowing down to images (Ex. 20:5; Deut. 5:9)

o   Worshipping images (Isa. 44:17; Dan. 3:5, 10, 15)

o   Sacrificing to images (Ps. 106:38; Acts 7:41)

o   Worshiping other gods (Ex. 22:20; Deut. 8:19; 30:17; 2 Kings 17:35; Ps. 81:9)

o   Swearing by other gods (Ex. 23:13; Josh. 23:7)

o   Speaking in the name of other gods (Deut. 18:20)

o   Looking to other gods (Hos. 3:1)

o   Serving other gods (Deut. 7:4; Jer. 5:19)

o   Worshiping the true God by an image (Ex. 32:4-6; Ps. 106:19-20)

o   Worshiping angels (Col. 2:18)

o   Worshiping celestial objects (Deut. 4:19; 17:3)

o   Worshiping demons (Matt. 4:9-10; Rev. 9:20)

o   Worshiping dead men (Ps. 106:28)

o   Setting up idols in the heart (Ezek. 14:3-4)

o   Covetousness (Eph. 5:5; Col. 3:5)

o   Sensuality (Phil. 3:19)[53]

As this list demonstrates, idolatry is far more than worshipping images made by hands; it includes worshipping substitutes for God erected in the heart. Fundamentally, *idols of the heart include anything we desire and find satisfaction in more than God.* Said differently, we become idolaters when our greatest joy is found in something other than God and we habitually yield ourselves to it until it defines our character. Eventually, a man becomes like the idol he serves—utterly worthless in rendering glory to God. The psalmist stated, "Those who make them will become like them, everyone who trusts in them" (Ps. 115:8).

IDOLATRY AS ADDICTION

The concept of idolatry is especially helpful for individuals battling what is commonly referred to as an "addiction"—a term that often abdicates personal responsibility by implying that a life-dominating sin is a "disease" rather than willful idolatry. They are "enslaved to various lusts and pleasures" (Titus 3:3). Notwithstanding the physical aspects of chemical addiction, Edward Welch rightly states that we should

> *acknowledge that addictions is a disorder of worship. By doing this we are not ignoring the out-of-control experience of addictions, and we are not being blinded by the complexities of an addict's inner world. However, we are gaining important insights into our hearts and our relationship with God. Such a view of change immediately reminds us that we are in a battle between the worship of God and the worship of ourselves and our desires.*[54]

The bottom line is that *we will never have victory over sin unless we depose the idols we allow to rule us.* We must become like Jonah who, while in the belly of the great fish, confessed that he had been deceived by sin. In deep contrition he confessed the core of his rebellion in a most enlightening statement: "They that observe lying vanities forsake their own mercies" (Jonah 2:8 KJV). Here we see the seductive and destructive nature of idolatry expressed in the phrase "lying vanities" that he "observed."[55]

Because Jonah hated the Assyrians for the savage atrocities they perpetrated upon his family and countrymen, he erected the idols of prejudice and revenge in his heart. Undoubtedly he worshipped these idols with silent acts of violence in his imagination and publicly vented his rage through curses and defamation. As a result, he forfeited God's blessing by tenaciously clinging to two self-serving lies, both of which stretch the bounds of naïveté to the breaking point.[56] First, he believed that his desire to have God destroy the Ninevites was righteous and therefore God's stated purpose to save them was wrong; and second, he believed he could flee from God.[57]

Though we would agree that Jonah's convictions were preposterous, Christians who unwittingly serve idols in their heart mirror his idiocy. Who could possibly believe that drunkenness or prescription drug abuse could result in anything other than hopeless desperation? Who could possibly believe that angry intimidation and incessant criticism could produce anything positive in a marriage? Yet people by the millions are slaves to these kinds of things! Why? *Because they are convinced their idols are the source of their deepest joy and they love them more than God!* They have no understanding of how "the grace of God has appeared . . . instructing us to deny ungodliness and worldly desires and to live sensibly, righteously and godly in the present age" (Titus 2:12).

TOPPLING IDOLS OF THE HEART

Having identified idols erected in the heart, pastors must admonish their flock in ways that are consistent with how God would have them defeated. What follows is a very brief threefold plan of attack worthy of much more specificity, especially as it may relate to individual situations, but beyond the scope of our discussion:

ADMONITION NUMBER ONE:
Detest them with a holy hatred.

We must begin by being brutally honest. We must identify anything we desire more than God and detest it. We must call sin by its right name and expose it for what it really is, not give it respectable names and titles and cloak it with sanitized euphemisms and hide behind "Christian liberty." Many are so fond of their sins they think liberty is threatened by censuring them. We must abhor that which God abhors and recognize the profound offense our substitute god is to the One true God and what an enormous danger our idol poses to our spiritual well-being. During the conquest of Canaan, God warned the Israelites of this danger. He warned them to share his hatred of the idols of the Canaanites saying, "You shall not bring an abomination into your house, and like it come under the ban; you shall utterly detest it and you shall utterly abhor it, for it is something banned" (Deut. 7:26).

We see the similar mindset in Paul's warnings to the Corinthians where he reminded them of God's warnings to Israel not to eat things sacrificed to pagan idols and thus to avoid any identification with the worship of demons. With this in mind he admonished the believers at Corinth: "What am I saying then? That an idol is anything, or what is offered to idols is anything? Rather, that the things which the Gentiles sacrifice they sacrifice to demons and not to God, and I do not want you to have fellowship with demons" (1 Cor. 10:19-20).

By detesting our heart idols with a holy hatred, we are agreeing with God. This is the heart of true confession. In 1 John 1:9 we are told, "If we confess our sins, He is faithful and righteous to forgive us our sins and to cleanse us from all unrighteousness." The word translated confess (*homologeo*) literally means "to say the same thing." When we agree with God about the heinousness of our idols and the sin they demand, we are well on our way to toppling them once and for all.

ADMONITION NUMBER TWO:
Flee from it.

The apostle Paul makes this so clear. "Therefore, my beloved, flee from idolatry." Here Paul underscores the danger of idolatry. As if an innocent child should reach for a venomous snake, he tells you to flee from an idol before it strikes. Like an ignorant child, you may not even know how dangerous it is. Most don't. Idols often fall under categories such as *prestige, people, possessions, pleasure, profit, or power.* If you find something in your life you desire more than God, anything that has become his substitute for worship, anything that is the all-consuming object of your time, affection, money, and thoughts, run from it as fast as you can. It's an idol.

John gives the same warning when he says, "Little children, guard yourselves from idols" (1 John 5:21). In this context he is speaking primarily of the idols of false beliefs and practices being taught by false teachers. These will inevitably lead us away from Christ, of whom John said, "This is the true God and eternal life" (v. 20). Any failure to flee from an idol is a dead giveaway that a man is still infatuated with what he should detest. This will only result in increased deception and slavery.

ADMONITION NUMBER THREE:
Avoid close contact with idolaters.

Defeating an idol of the heart requires a decisive commitment to this third admonition. To detest an idol with a holy hatred and flee from it will be of little benefit for a man who remains in close relationship with those who worship a false god. Like placing a good apple in a barrel of rotten apples, he will eventually become like the rest. Once again, the apostle Paul makes this abundantly clear: "But actually, I wrote to you not to associate with any so-called brother if he should be an immoral person, or covetous, or an idolater, or a reviler, or a drunkard, or a swindler—not even to eat with such a one" (1 Cor. 5:11). This is the extent to which we should separate from such people.

Paul sounds warnings that often go unheeded: "Do not be deceived: 'Bad company corrupts good morals'" (1 Cor. 15:33); "Do not participate in the unfruitful deeds of darkness, but instead even expose them" (Eph. 5:11). Yet many participate vicariously through the various forms of entertainment they choose to indulge in.

This is a message the church needs to hear. Far too often evangelicals have a cavalier attitude toward sin in the lives of other professing members of their own church and refuse to disassociate themselves from them (2 Thess. 3:6, 14, 15). The result is devastating. The leaven ends up leavening the whole lump. And it is the role of a faithful pastor to warn against this danger with great specificity, clarity, and conviction.

This is at the heart of biblical shepherding. While individual problems will vary greatly, sin is always sin, and the central truths of the gospel are always the answer. It is the solemn responsibility of every pastor to help his people understand the severity and scope of their idolatry and their sinful allegiances to them. Only then will they know what they need to *put off* and *put on* (Col. 3:5-17) in order to bridge the chasm between the old self and the new self.

ADMONITION NUMBER FOUR:
Kill Your Sin

God would have our love for him constrain us to renounce and kill sin: "If you are living according to the flesh, you must die; but if by the Spirit you are putting to death the deeds of the body, you will live" (Rom. 8:13). Few believers see the need to be constantly killing the remaining influences of the flesh through the power of the indwelling Spirit who energizes our sanctification. When we kill something, we deprive it of its strength, energy, and power to exert itself. We must never feed our idol-worshipping lusts, but starve them, as we would starve cancer cells to prevent them from growing.

But we must not only mortify the lusts of the flesh, but also replace our lusts and grow in the opposite graces: "Let us cleanse ourselves from all defilement of flesh and spirit, perfecting holiness in the fear of God" (2 Cor. 7:1). Without a decisive commitment to personal holiness, worse tenants will soon reoccupy a house that is merely swept clean (Luke 11:25-26). If we are to walk in the power of holiness, we must not only avoid sin, and even the appearance of sin, but we must "be holy as He is holy." The grace of God not only teaches us to "deny ungodliness and worldly desires," but "to live sensibly, righteously and godly in this present age" (Titus 2:12).

SHEPHERDING PRIORITY NUMBER THREE:
WE MUST TEACH OTHERS THE IMPORTANCE OF INTIMACY WITH GOD THAT LEADS TO MATURITY.

While "admonishing" (*noutheteo*) denotes warning, exhorting, encouraging, or correcting, "teaching" (*didasko*) carries many of the same implications, but with the added emphasis of *imparting practical doctrinal truth* "with all wisdom, so that we may present every man complete in Christ" (v. 28). Once again, Paul was committed to this one end. This was the passion of his heart and the goal of his ministry. He wanted them to be "filled with the knowledge of His will . . . increasing in the knowledge of God" (Col. 1:9-10), which will inevitably lead to an increasing love for him, his word, and his people.

Likewise, he prayed for the saints at Ephesus, that "the God of our Lord Jesus Christ, the Father of glory, may give to you a spirit of wisdom and of revelation in the knowledge of Him" (Eph. 1:17). And most importantly, he prayed that they would have a profound understanding of the Lord Jesus Christ "in whom are hidden all the treasures of wisdom and knowledge" (Col. 2:3). Every pastor must be equally devoted to teaching Christian theology and helping his flock attain to the knowledge of the truth (1 Tim. 2:4; 2 Tim. 2:25; Titus 1:1).

But we must understand that learning Bible doctrine through expository preaching and the study of systematic theology is an exercise in futility unless it is accompanied by a prayerful commitment to grow into the likeness of God in character and conduct. We must pray that our people will plead with God for an ever-deepening relationship with the Lover of their soul. This is what Jesus had in mind in his parable of the vine and the branches (John 15:1-11). As believers we will never experience the love and joy of intimate fellowship with God unless we *abide in Christ.*

Jesus spoke of the need for intimate fellowship, promising that as a result, "My joy may be in you, and *that* your joy may be made full" (John 15:9-11). What a magnificent truth: *the Spirit generates an exhilarating, felt joy in the consciousness of the abiding believer.* Paul expressed it as "the love of God poured out within our hearts through the Holy Spirit who was given to us" (Rom. 5:5), and Peter described this as "joy inexpressible and full of glory" (1 Peter 1:8). No one who enjoys such a level of intimate fellowship with Christ will ever have a lack of adoration for the majesty and holiness of God.

LABORING FOR SPIRITUAL MATURITY

As we shall see in the next chapter, Paul worked to the point of exhaustion to see people grow into spiritual maturity. Because of his great love for Christ and his church, he said, "For this purpose also I labor, striving according to His power, which mightily works within me" (Col. 1:29; cf. 2:1-7). He expressed this again in chapter two when he said,

> For I want you to know how great a struggle I have
> on your behalf and for those who are at Laodicea,

and for all those who have not personally seen
my face, that their hearts may be encouraged,
having been knit together in love, and attaining to
all the wealth that comes from the full assurance
of understanding, resulting in a true knowledge
of God's mystery, that is, Christ Himself, in
whom are hidden all the treasures of wisdom and
knowledge. I say this so that no one will delude
you with persuasive argument. For even though I
am absent in body, nevertheless I am with you in
spirit, rejoicing to see your good discipline and the
stability of your faith in Christ. Therefore as you
have received Christ Jesus the Lord, so walk in Him,
having been firmly rooted and now being built up in
Him and established in your faith, just as you were
instructed, and overflowing with gratitude.

(Col. 2:1-7)

While the fruit of spiritual maturity will naturally grow on the vine of genuine saving faith, the Father will use the under-shepherds of Christ to help him prune that vine that it might bear more fruit (John 15:1-17). This will require the same kind of labor and struggle that we see in Paul's life and ministry. We must ask ourselves as pastors, "Do I labor and struggle on behalf of my flock, that I may 'present every man complete in Christ'?" In the passage above, Paul even gives us an abbreviated list of what this would include:

○ A heart that is strengthened by the Holy Spirit to courageously endure the difficulties of life and enjoy all that is theirs in Christ Jesus (2:2a).

○ A fervency in self-sacrificing love for God and fellow believers in the body of Christ (2:2b).

○ A complete understanding and application of biblical truth that leads to the assurance of salvation and confidence in the truths of the gospel, especially the deity and sufficiency of Christ (2c-5).

○ A walk with Christ that manifests a living union *with* him and an increasing likeness *to* him (6-7a).

○ A heart that overflows with gratitude to God as the gracious and glorious Author of all the blessings of his saving grace (7b).

We see it as well in the life an English Puritan pastor of the Church at Kidderminster, Richard Baxter (1615–1691). His ministry truly embodied a man who was *committed to the one end of presenting every man complete in Christ* (Col. 1:28). I offer one small portion of his autobiography (originally published in 1655 under the title: *Gildas Salvianus: The Reformed Pastor*) as both an exhortation (as it continues to be to me) and a source of encouragement to every pastor who is serious about the charge. "Be on guard for yourselves and for all the flock, among which the Holy Spirit has made you overseers, to shepherd the church of God which He purchased with His own blood" (Acts 20:28). Baxter understood what was required to "admonish the unruly, encourage the fainthearted, help the weak, be patient with everyone" (1 Thess. 5:14). He understood that true gospel ministry is more than public preaching; it also requires private shepherding. Of his ministry, he said,

We spend Monday and Tuesday, from morning almost to night, in the work, taking about fifteen or sixteen families in a week, that we may go through the parish, in which there are upwards of eight hundred families, in a year; and I cannot say yet that one family hath refused to come to me, and but few persons excused themselves, and shifted it off. And I find more outward signs of success with most that do come, than from all my public preaching to them.[58]

While it is easy to dismiss his ministry model of biblical shepherding as one that is not suited for our modern day, I would humbly caution against such a response. To be sure, the society and culture of seventeenth-century England is very different in many ways than in our modern day. But do not kid yourself: sin is just as much sin today as it was then. The gospel is just as powerful today as it was then. And godly pastors committed to face-to-face shepherding are just as needed today as they were then.

Perhaps the words of Baxter himself will humble and inspire every reader as they continue to do for me.

It is too common for men to think that the work of the ministry is nothing but to preach, and to baptize, and to administer the Lord's supper, and to visit the sick. By this means the people will submit to no more; and too many ministers are such strangers to their own calling, that they will do no more. It hath oft grieved my heart to observe some eminent able preachers, how little they do for the saving of souls, save only in the pulpit; and to how little purpose much of their labour is, by this neglect. They have hundreds of people that they never spoke a word to personally for their salvation; and if we may judge by their practice, they consider it not as their duty; and the principal thing that hardeneth men in this oversight is the common neglect of the private part of the work by others. There are so few that do much in it, and the omission hath grown so common among pious, able men, that the disgrace of it is abated by their ability; and a man may now be guilty of it without any particular notice or dishonour. Never doth sin so reign in a church or state, as when it hath gained reputation, or, at least, is no disgrace to the sinner, nor a matter of offence to beholders. But I make no doubt, through the mercy of God, that the restoring of the practice of personal oversight will convince many ministers, that this is as truly their work as that which they now do, and may awaken them to see that the ministry is another kind of business than too many excellent preachers take it to be.

Brethren, do but set yourselves closely to this work, and follow it diligently; and though you do it silently, without any words to them that are negligent, I am in hope that most of you who are present may live to see the day, when the neglect of private personal oversight of all the flock shall be taken for a scandalous and odious omission, and shall be as disgraceful to them that are guilty of it, as preaching but once a day was heretofore. A schoolmaster must take a personal account of his scholars, or else he is like to do little good. If physicians should only read a public lecture on physic, their patients would not be much the better of them; nor would a lawyer secure your estate by reading a lecture on law. Now, the charge of a pastor requireth personal dealing, as well as any of these. Let us show the world this by our practice; for most men are grown regardless of bare words.[59]

Final Word

I fear the role of biblical shepherding is foreign to most pastors. Most Christians will admit that they have experienced very little of anything like the kind of intentional, personal involvement described in this chapter. Having grown up in the church, I must admit that I seldom had any one-on-one, face-to-face encounters with a pastor or any other church leader, unless I initiated it. And I cannot remember a single time when a pastor or elder came to visit our family simply to check up on us and see how we were doing spiritually and how he could minister to us. Fellowship was always at a distance, and the concept of really being shepherded was foreign to me, as it is to most people.

However, as a pastor, I know how hard it is to find time to do this, and it requires some creative maneuvering and scheduling to make it happen. But whether it's over a casual cup of coffee, or during an accidental (providential) encounter at the grocery store, or during a fellowship meal at the church, taking advantage of every opportunity to invest our lives in our people will always be met with enthusiasm and bear much fruit in their lives as well as in ours.

May I encourage every pastor and church leader to be equally dedicated to his flock, *committed to the one end* of "presenting every man complete in Christ," consistent with the lyrics of a familiar hymn that should resonate in our hearts:

RISE UP, O MEN OF GOD!

Rise up, O men of God!
Have done with lesser things.
Give heart and mind and soul and strength
To serve the King of kings.

Rise up, O men of God!
The kingdom tarries long.
Bring in the day of brotherhood
And end the night of wrong.

Rise up, O men of God!
The church for you doth wait,
Her strength unequal to her task;
Rise up, and make her great!

Lift high the cross of Christ!
Tread where his feet have trod.
As brothers of the Son of Man,
Rise up, O men of God!

William Pierson Merrill (1867–1954)

CHAPTER 7

KEY PRINCIPLE SEVEN: CONFIRMED BY ONE POWER

*"For this purpose also I labor, striving according
to His power, which mightily works within me."*

Colossians 1:29

It has been my observation that there exists a marked difference among evangelical pastors. I am not referring to distinctions in Bible doctrine and theological positions, though they exist. Nor am I referring to variations in philosophy of ministry and preaching styles, which will inevitably differ according to culture, theology, spiritual giftedness, and overall personality. My observation has to do with *character*, the dissimilarity between the *mediocre* and the *exceptional*, the *weak* and the *strong*, the *ineffective* and the *effective*, the *immature* and the *mature*. Very few have what I would call a *godly presence* about them.

By *godly presence* I mean a man with a noticeable aura of godliness about him, both in and out of the pulpit—a man like Jesus; a man who possesses a palpable sense of humility and love that draws you into his presence; a man who exudes spiritual strength, confidence, boldness, wisdom, and a noticeable fervency that marks him as a man of God, and a man on a mission; a man so lost in the wonder of the majesty of God, so filled by the Divine presence, that nothing in this world causes him to despair or tempts him to distraction. This is that rare man whose authority enters a room with him and commands respect without ever asking for it.

I am speaking of that extraordinary man who is "full of the Spirit and of wisdom" (Acts 6:3), the qualifications the early saints were to look for in choosing the first deacons, virtues not every man possesses. A man who "in speech, conduct, love, faith *and* purity, [shows himself] an example of those who believe" (1 Tim. 4:12), what Paul called a "man of God" (1 Tim. 6:11).

This is that exceptional man who has such a great likeness to Jesus that he actually emanates his power in ways that are mysteriously transcendent and profoundly influential. He manifests what Paul described as "the surpassing greatness of His power toward us who believe ... in accordance with the working of the strength of His might" (Eph. 1:19); a personal power that only comes from "Him who is able to do far more abundantly beyond all that we ask or think, according to the power that works within us" (3:20).

I have not known many such men, and I can only pray to become one. But when I have been around them, or heard them preach, or read what they have written, I instantly sense a *godly presence* that comes only from the unrestricted rule of the Spirit of God in that man's heart. They are the kind of men you want at your side when you go into battle.

To be sure, there exists a continuum in this realm of spiritual maturity, but few men who stand behind pulpits today rise to that manifestation of Christlikeness. In fact, I fear most pastors are far more sizzle than steak—more form than substance. I have lived long enough to hear many of them preach, from the *crier* to the *comedian*; from the *actor* to the *monotone*; from the *angry* to the *saccharine*; from the *orator* to the *stammerer*; from the *screamer* to the *stupid*, from the *exegete* with his self-promoting erudition to the *biblical counselor* who tortures every text to find something to "put off" or "put on."

I have personally endured the *voice quiverer*, the *chicken walker*, the *pulpit pounder*, the *heresy hunter*, the *iconoclastic hipster*, the *preference pusher*, and the *perpetual fundraiser*. But it is very rare to encounter a man with *godly presence* who can simply open up the Word of God with divine authority, disappear behind "the light of the glory of God in the face of Christ" (2 Cor. 4:6), and with convicting power bring men and women, young and old, into the presence of the Most High God.

There are many examples of such men in Scripture, like Peter and John in Acts 4, who, because of their confidence, boldness, and knowledge beyond their training, amazed the Sanhedrists who "began to recognize them as having been with Jesus" (v. 13). There are men like Stephen, "a man full of faith and the Holy Spirit" (Acts 6:5), "full of grace and power ... doing great wonders and signs among the people" (v. 8), whose "face was like the face of an angel" (v. 15) and who prayed for God to forgive his murderers (7:60).

There are men like the apostle Paul through whom God "worked unusual miracles" (Acts 19:11), whose bold preaching caused a wicked ruler to tremble (Acts 24:25); a man who "preached boldly in the name of the Lord" to those who wanted to kill him (Acts 9:28-29). Paul was truly a determined soldier of the cross, constantly engaged in "the defense and confirmation of the gospel" (Phil. 1:7), a man who stood courageously before Caesar himself, the most powerful ruler in the world, and bravely gave his testimony of faith in Christ (Acts 28:17-31)—a man who, despite enormous opposition, "fought the good fight

. . . finished the race" and "kept the faith" (2 Tim. 4:7).

All the godly men of Scripture understood what Paul meant when he said, "For this purpose also I labor, *striving according to His power, which mightily works within me*" (Col. 1:29, emphasis mine).

LABORING AND STRIVING IN THE SPIRIT

As shepherds, we can learn much from Paul's example. He was committed to "[presenting] every man complete in Christ" (Col. 1:28b), so much so that he went on to add, "For this purpose also I labor" (v. 29). The term "labor" (Greek: *kopiao*) means to work to the point of exhaustion. "In wider Greek *kopos* means 'beating,'" as James Dunn comments, "the weariness that results from being repeatedly struck, and so by analogy the physical tiredness caused by work and exertion."[60] When it came to preaching and ministry, Paul gave it his all, regardless of the circumstances in which he found himself; the resumé of his ministry experiences underscore the profound difficulties in which he labored (2 Cor. 11:23-28).

Not only did he "labor" to the point of exhaustion; he also described his efforts as "striving according to His power, which mightily works within me." The term "striving" (Greek: *agonizomai*), is used in the context of engaging in an athletic contest (see 1 Cor. 9:25). This underscores the need for self-discipline and the exertion of maximum effort. When encouraging Timothy to "discipline [himself] for the purpose of godliness" (1 Tim. 4:7), Paul used the combination of both of these terms: "For it is for this we *labor* and *strive*, because we have fixed our hope on the living God" (v. 10, emphasis mine).

But Paul's *laboring* and *striving* were utterly dependent upon God's enablement through the power of his indwelling Spirit: "But by the grace of God I am what I am, and His grace toward me did not prove vain; but I labored even more than all of them, yet not I, but the grace of God with me" (1 Cor. 15:10).

Paul understood what it meant to be "filled with the Spirit" (Eph. 5:18). A literal translation of the Greek verb "be filled," *plerousthe*, carries the idea of "be being kept filled," expressed elsewhere as the process of "walking by the Spirit" (Gal. 5:18). Furthermore, since "be filled" is in the passive voice, we as believers are the ones receiving the action. And what is that? *It is the Holy Spirit's continuous and complete spiritual control of our lives so we can walk in perfect harmony with the will of God and be empowered for his service.* By using the imperative, Paul commands us to *continue* being filled or controlled by the Holy Spirit. When we do, we manifest the fruit of the Spirit (vv. 22-23). This is what Paul had in mind in a parallel passage:

> *Let the word of Christ richly dwell within you, with*
> *all wisdom teaching and admonishing one another*
> *with psalms and hymns and spiritual songs, singing*
> *with thankfulness in your hearts to God. Whatever*
> *you do in word or deed, do all in the name of the Lord*
> *Jesus, giving thanks through Him to God the Father.*
> *(Col. 3:16-17)*

Paul truly practiced what he preached. This is why he was so effective in his *laboring* and *striving.* He was confirmed by one power: *the Holy Spirit who controlled him.* He continuously submitted to the Holy Spirit's control and providences. If you are a pastor, it is imperative that you follow Paul's example so you, too, can "labor, striving according to His power, which mightily works within [you]" (Col. 1:29).

We have all witnessed pastors who operate in the flesh rather than the Spirit. Their character is like their preaching: boring, shallow, and ineffective. The fruit of the Spirit is sparse and sickly on the vine of their life. Like butchers, they *drive* their sheep rather than *lead* them like shepherds. They are constantly exerting their authority because most people do not naturally follow them as trusted leaders. They *demand* respect rather than *enjoy* it. Very few people want to be like them. They are *endured* more than *esteemed*, *tolerated* more than *appreciated*, and *ignored* more than *heeded.* For the most part, though they may be immensely popular with vast congregations, they are weak and spiritually fruitless, bereft of *godly presence.* Why? *Because they are not Spirit-controlled*; they are not surrendering to him on a moment-by-moment basis as he has revealed himself in his Word. Not so the apostle Paul, that choice servant of God whom we should all imitate. In fact, he has asked us to do so: "Be imitators of me, just as I also am of Christ" (1 Cor. 11:1).

CHRIST'S DEPENDENCE UPON THE HOLY SPIRIT

Our supreme example of a man with *godly presence* is, of course, our Savior and Lord, the God-man Jesus Christ. Although he was the Son of God, he, too, was *Spirit-controlled.* In his incarnation, he was totally dependent upon the ministry of the Holy Spirit in all things, including his virgin conception and birth (Luke 1:34-35), his baptism (Luke 3:21-22), his temptation in the wilderness (Luke 4:1), his preaching (Luke 4:17-21), his crucifixion (Heb. 9:14), and his resurrection (Rom. 1:4; 8:11). It was the Holy Spirit who empowered him (Luke 4:14-15), filled him (John 3:34), and led him in ministry (Acts 1:2). The Spirit's role in his life was foretold in Isaiah's prophecies (Isa. 11:2-3; 42:1; 61:1-3).

We must remember that in his incarnation, the Son of God was fully God as well as fully human. And because of his humanity, he was utterly dependent upon the ministry of the Holy Spirit in every area of his life and ministry. Think of what that entailed. Though equal to God, our precious Savior voluntarily surrendered his preincarnate glories that he might become like us. As the supreme representative of mankind, he alone could fulfill our original purpose in glorifying God in perfect obedience, yet he alone could suffer and die in our place.

For this reason, the writer of Hebrews says, "But we do see Him who was made for a little while lower than the angels, namely, Jesus, because of the suffering of death crowned with glory and honor, so that by the grace of God He might taste death for everyone" (Heb. 2:9). He "had to be made like His brethren in all things, so that He might become a merciful and faithful high priest in things pertaining to God, to make propitiation for the sins of the people" (Heb. 2:17).

The One whom angels worship had to leave the grandeur of heaven and descend to this earth, to a place that reeked with the stench of sewage and body odor. He had to live on a planet corrupted by sin, ruled by Satan, and polluted by death. Though he totally possessed his divine nature, attributes, and prerogatives, he voluntarily surrendered the independent exercise of his divine attributes to do the will of his Father as stated in Philippians 2:6-7:

> *Although He existed in the form of God, did not*
> *regard equality with God a thing to be grasped,*
> *but emptied Himself, taking the form of a bond-*
> *servant, and being made in the likeness of men.*
> *Being found in appearance as a man, He humbled*
> *Himself by becoming obedient to the point of*
> *death, even death on a cross.*

Jesus could never have endured all these things apart from the ministry of the Holy Spirit. Surely, if there had been another way to redeem sinful human beings, God would have done it. But this was the way he chose, the perfect way, the most glorious way.

Because God is holy, all sin must be punished. But sinful people could never atone for their own sin, so "when the fullness of the time came, God sent forth His Son, born of a woman, born under the Law, so that He might redeem those who were under the Law, that we might receive the adoption as sons" (Gal. 4:4-5). So Jesus had to take upon himself the nature of man in order to be punished for our sin, yet he also had to be God in order to endure the sufferings of all the elect, a punishment only God could endure. The work of redemption demanded a *theanthropon*, a God-man—One in whom the human nature and the Godhead were inseparably joined together in one Person.

Jesus was the offspring of David according to the flesh, yet as God, a ruler whose goings forth are from eternity (Mic. 5:2). As a man he had to die as our substitute, but only an omniscient God could intimately know all whom the Father had given him and bear their sins in his body specifically in an actual, (not potential) atonement. A perfect man had to die, but only God is holy. Human flesh had to go to the grave, but only God could overcome it. God's holy and infinite justice could not be satisfied apart from a holy and infinite ransom, and only by his own provision could such a remedy be accomplished. So both the human and divine natures had to be supernaturally woven together by the Holy Spirit, resulting in the virgin birth of the Lord Jesus Christ.

My point is simply this: *in the humiliation of his incarnation, the Lord Jesus Christ was utterly dependent upon the ministry of the Holy Spirit to enable his human nature to be victorious over the temptations of sin and Satan, endure the cross, and be raised from the dead.* Only then could he fully accomplish the work of redemption the Father had sent him to do. If the Son of God relied totally upon the Holy Spirit in his life, should we not do likewise? Should we not live in his presence in a state of perpetual communion, seeking every expression of his goodness and grace?

A CALL TO PRAYER

The rigors of ministry are grueling and time consuming. I have not had anything less than a fifty-hour week over the course of my pastoral ministry. We are on call 24/7. Add to that family needs, a little recreation, some yard upkeep, and regular exercise, and before you know it we are exhausted. But sadly, without realizing it, the first thing that gets eliminated from our busy schedule is the most important: *our private pursuit of holiness through prayer.*

This act of worship must never be seen as a legalistic *duty*, but as a passionate *desire*—a joyful *discipline*—like eating a great meal; a longing to see God glorified and experience his soul-satisfying presence deep within us. We must remember that prayer not only demonstrates our great need for help, but also our confidence in the resources of his goodness and grace, and God is greatly honored by our trust in him. What father fails to rejoice in the opportunity to express his benevolence to his child crying out in need? The psalmist summarized God's attitude in this regard, "Call upon me in the day of trouble; I will deliver you, and you shall glorify me" (Ps. 50:15, RSV). John Piper adds this helpful observation:

> *Jesus said to aim at two things in prayer: your joy and God's glory. "Ask and you will receive, so that your joy may be made full" (John 16:24). "Whatever you ask in My name, that will I do, so that the Father may be glorified in the Son" (John 14:13). These are not two aims, but one. When we delight ourselves in the Lord, the Lord is glorified in giving the desires of our heart. (Ps. 37:4)[61]*

The incarnate Son of God is our supreme example in this very thing. In Mark 1:35 we read: "In the morning, while it was still dark, Jesus got up, left the house, and went away to a secluded place, and was praying there." Pre-dawn private worship was the habit of our Savior. Is it yours? There is perhaps no better gauge of a man's spiritual maturity than his secret devotion to God in prayer. Show me a man lax in private prayer, and I will show you a spiritual infant. It matters little how long he has known Christ or how long he has been a pastor. If he has no secret devotion to God in private worship, he remains in a stage of spiritual immaturity. He fails to grasp the majesty and holiness of God that deserves our utmost worship in prayer. Moreover, he fails to see how God is honored by his trust in his infinite resources and how he delights in meeting his needs as a loving heavenly Father.

In his sermon, *The Most High A Prayer-Hearing God*, Jonathan Edwards (1703–1758) preached on this issue in the context of "a fast appointed on the account of epidemical sickness at the eastward of Boston." His text was: "O thou that hearest prayer" (Psalm 65:2). Here is a small part of what he said:

Why is God so ready to hear the prayers of men?—To this I answer . . . because he is a God of infinite grace and mercy. It is indeed a very wonderful thing, that so great a God should be so ready to hear our prayers, though we are so despicable and unworthy. That he should give free access at all times to everyone, should allow us to be importunate without esteeming it an indecent boldness, [and] should be so rich in mercy to them that call upon him: that worms of the dust should have such power with God by prayer, that he should do such great things in answer to their prayers, and should show himself, as it were, overcome by them. This is very wonderful, when we consider the distance between God and us, and how we have provoked him by our sins, and how unworthy we are of the least gracious notice. It cannot be from any need that God stands in of us, for our goodness extends not to him. Neither can it be from anything in us to incline the heart of God to us. It cannot be from any worthiness in our prayers, which are in themselves polluted things. But it is because God delights in mercy and condescension. He is herein infinitely distinguished from all other Gods. He is the great fountain of all good, from whom goodness flows as light from the sun.[62]

Knowing, as Edwards says, "God delights in mercy and condescension," can there be any greater reason to petition him in prayer? "He delights in unchanging love" (Mic. 7:18). The blessings we receive from his beneficence must then be considered secondary when compared to the glory he receives in giving. Nevertheless, the answers he gives to our prayers are always rich beyond measure, always perfect, suited and timed to accomplish his purposes in us and for his name's sake. Like Moses, just being in the presence of the Lord for an extended period of time causes our face, as it were, to reflect the radiance of his glory.

For this reason I say, again, any pastor without a private prayer life will lack power in ministry and will certainly not manifest a *godly presence*. The theme of Christ will seldom be prominent in his conversations because it is not dominant in his heart. In fact, I have never met a pastor with a robust private prayer life who struggles with things like debilitating depression, addictions, or some life-dominating sin. I have never heard a wife offer a legitimate complaint about her husband who is faithful in private prayer. I have never heard a child weep in fear and frustration over a father who lives in a state of intimate communion with God, faithful to, "Rejoice always; pray without ceasing; in everything give thanks; for this is God's will for you in Christ Jesus" (1 Thess. 5:16-18).

Let me ask you this question: Do you only pray before meals or do you ever pray before dawn? For most, prayer is limited to meals, or when some great crisis comes into their life. But sadly, far too many pastors are unfamiliar with the mercy seat, strangers to the throne of grace. Communing with the lover of their souls is just not a priority, because he is not the source of their greatest satisfaction and joy.

While a lack of self-discipline contributes to this laxity, it is primarily a consequence of loving other things more than God. Some idol has taken the place of God and distracted a man from this essential discipline and privilege. Frankly, no ministry will be effective, no marriage will be fulfilling, no family will ever be blessed apart from the pleadings of private prayer. To be sure, prayer will never be the early dawn priority of the sluggard who likes to sleep in, nor will it be the priority of the Sunday morning pastor who pretends to be serving Christ for a few hours on Sunday, but the rest of the week lives for himself. But it will be the priority of the battle-weary soldier of the cross in desperate need of strength—that warrior who begs for more discernment, faith, endurance, humility, love, patience, and fruit—who pleads for more light in the Word and boldness in battle, because he knows that apart from Christ, he can do nothing (John 15:5).

I confess that, as a pastor, one of my greatest regrets is that I spent too much time in public ministry and not enough time in private communion with the Lord. But over the years I have learned that *prayer* is more important than *preparation*; the *closet* is more important than the *library*; and the *heart* is more important than *knowledge*. I have learned that prayer is the spade that unearths hidden jewels in a text. It is the drill that bores deep into the caverns of living water. I have learned that prayer is what calls forth the Spirit to give life to the spiritually dead and dissolve hardened hearts. I have learned that it is prayer that ignites a preacher with holy zeal and transforms his clumsy rhetoric into tongues of fire. I have learned that it is prayer—disciplined, fervent, private, persistent prayer—that transforms weak, shallow, cowardly pastors into mighty warriors of the Cross.

Many people today are starving for the glory and greatness of God, and they are looking to godly men with a godly presence to show him to them. And we are the men God has chosen to shepherd them. But we cannot do this under our own power. No matter how cluttered and chaotic life might get, we must make it a disciplined, non-negotiable, uninterrupted priority to go hard after God in our own personal, private pursuit of holiness. Our secret devotion to him is more important than anything else in life and ministry. We must long for the *felt presence* of Christ, and pray earnestly for it. Only when we experience his glorious perfections can we compel others to *seek* him and *see* him in his Word. Only then can we create a real thirst for the living God in our people.

This must be the preoccupation of our heart in sermon preparation, long before we stand in the pulpit. We must

*learn the power of prayer if we ever hope to lead others
to Christ and "present every man complete in Christ"
(Col. 1:28). This is what unleashes "His power, which
mightily works within [us]" (v. 29). New England Pastor
Phillips Brooks (1835–1893) said it best: Nothing but fire
kindles fire. To know in one's whole nature what it is to
live by Christ; to be His, not our own; to be so occupied
with gratitude for what He did for us and for what He
continually is to us that His will and His glory shall be the
sole desires of our life ... that is the first necessity of the
preacher.[63]*

Similarly, Dr. David Larsen, professor Emeritus of Preaching
at Trinity Evangelical Divinity School—truly a man with *godly
presence* who speaks with the power of the Holy Spirit—said
this about prayer and preaching:

*Strange it is that any discussion of preaching should take
place outside the context of believing prayer. We have not
prepared until we have.... We cannot represent God if
we have not stood before God. It is more important for me
therefore to teach a student to pray than to preach.[64]*

A CALL TO PIETY

The apostle Paul was confirmed by one power, the power
of the Holy Spirit, that power that worked mightily within
him (Col. 1:29). We must likewise be so persuaded of our
own inability and so desperate for the Spirit's power in and
through us, that we cast ourselves completely upon him in utter
dependence. It is this spirit of private *prayer*, combined with
personal *piety* that precedes blessing in our preaching of the
gospel. This is the means by which we protect ourselves from
the snares of the evil one, which will be more numerous and
dangerous than those he sets for the average Christian. The wise
Puritan pastor, Richard Baxter, warned of this very thing:

*Take heed to yourselves, because the tempter will more
ply you with his temptations than other men. If you will
be the leaders against the prince of darkness, he will spare*

*you no further than God restraineth him. He beareth the
greatest malice to those that are engaged to do him the
greatest mischief. As he hateth Christ more than any of us,
because he is the General of the field, the Captain of our
salvation, and doth more than all the world besides against
his kingdom; so doth he hate the leaders under him, more
than the common soldiers: he knows what a rout he may
make among them, if the leaders fall before their eyes. . . .
Take heed, therefore, brethren, for the enemy hath a special
eye upon you. You shall have his most subtle insinuations,
and incessant solicitations, and violent assaults. As wise
and learned as you are, take heed to yourselves, lest he
outwit you. The devil is a greater scholar than you, and
a nimble disputant: he can transform himself into an
angel of light to deceive: he will get within you, and trip
up your heels before you are aware: he will play the juggle
with you undiscerned, and cheat you of your faith or
innocency, and you shall not know that you have lost it;
nay, he will make you believe it is multiplied or increased,
when it is lost. You shall see neither hook nor line, much
less the subtle angel himself, while he is offering you his
bait. And his bait shall be so fitted to your temper and
disposition, that he will be sure to find advantages within
you, and make your own principles and inclination betray
you; and whenever he ruineth you, he will make you the
instruments of ruin to others.*[65]

One of the most frightening characteristics of our
unredeemed humanness is our inability to spot spiritual danger
in our life. Even as pastors, we are much better at spotting the
concealed landmines in the paths of others than in the ones
we walk every day. We are notoriously weak when it comes to
Jesus' warning, "Keep watching and praying that you may not
enter into temptation; the spirit is willing, but the flesh is weak"
(Matt. 26:41). I fear pride is the biggest culprit. Knowing "pride
goes before destruction, and a haughty spirit before stumbling"
(Prov. 16:18), and knowing the enemy seeks our destruction more
than all others, we must be all the more vigilant. Our constant
prayer must be, "Search me, O God, and know my heart; try me
and know my anxious thoughts; and see if there be any hurtful

way in me, and lead me in the everlasting way" (Ps. 139:23-24).

We must learn what it is to live *coram Deo* ("in the presence of God") and plead with him for protection and power. This is the only way we can "stand firm against the schemes of the devil" (Eph. 6:11). In that context, Paul went on to say, "With all prayer and petition pray at all times in the Spirit, and with this in view, be on the alert with all perseverance and petition for all the saints" (Eph. 6:18). This is what unleashes the Spirit's power within us and produces a *godly presence* that both reflects and emanates the glory of God. Only then are we the kind of men God can use. Paul addressed this in his exhortation to Timothy when he said,

> *Therefore, if anyone cleanses himself from these
> things, he will be a vessel for honor, sanctified,
> useful to the Master, prepared for every good
> work. Now flee from youthful lusts and pursue
> righteousness, faith, love and peace, with those
> who call on the Lord from a pure heart.*
>
> *(2 Tim. 2:21)*

Whenever I counsel fellow pastors who are struggling with some sin issue in their life, I always ask them to describe their walk with Christ. More often than not their answer reveals a great deficiency in piety. Their private life does not accurately reflect their public life. Self-gratification is often more important than self-denial. This is especially prevalent in our lax evangelical culture that has little regard for personal holiness and seldom sees sufficient cause for a man to be disqualified from ministry. With such a low standard for righteousness, few pastors share Paul's fear of disqualification and his commitment to self-discipline to guard himself from it: "I discipline my body and make it my slave, so that, after I have preached to others, I myself will not be disqualified" (1 Cor. 9:27).

When was the last time you even heard of, much less attended, a major seminar on godliness for pastors and church leaders? How many best-selling books address reverence for God in the inner man, the kind of piety that produces righteous behavior in Christians, especially pastors? Too many men simply do not guard their heart and heed Paul's admonition to "cleanse ourselves from all defilement of flesh and spirit, perfecting holiness in the fear of God" (2 Cor. 7:1). If this is you, I urge you to get serious about guarding your own heart. For I assure you, the enemy is already working a plan to defeat you.

During a season of prayer and fasting, the godly Scottish pastor, Robert Murray McCheyne, recorded this in his journal:

> *Is it the desire of my heart to be made altogether holy? Is there any sin I wish to retain? Lord, thou knowest all things; thou knowest that I hate all sin, and desire to be made altogether like Thee. It is the sweetest word in the Bible, "Sin shall not have dominion over you." Oh, then, that I might lie low in the dust!*[66]

With such a commitment to personal holiness, which was well documented throughout his life and ministry, we should seriously heed his warning to pastors:

> *Do not forget the culture of the inner man—I mean of the heart. How diligently the cavalry officer keeps his sabre clean and sharp; every stain he rubs off with the greatest care. Remember you are God's sword, His instrument—I trust a chosen vessel unto Him to bear His name. In great measure, according to the purity and perfections of the instrument, will be the success. It is not great talents God blesses so much as great likeness to Jesus. A holy minister is an awful weapon in the hand of God.*[67]

This is the kind of heart we must cultivate as pastors if we ever expect to be confirmed by the same power as that of the apostle Paul. This is what will produce within us the confident assurance that we are God's man doing God's work. This is what will protect us from becoming a compromising people-pleaser instead of a man with *godly presence* that radiates the qualities of Christ we cherish in our soul. In his address on "The Minister as a Man," D. Martyn Lloyd-Jones spoke most pointedly to this issue:

> *This matter is difficult and may seem uninteresting but it is vitally important. The ruling idea ought to be that the pastor*

*is a shepherd, not a pet lamb. He must be alert to the danger
of trying to be nice and popular and chatty. The minister
is to be always and everywhere "the man of God" and not
merely when he is in chapel or taking a service. It is our duty
to remember our calling. The minister should always move
amongst the people as one who has been with God. His chief
object should be to please God rather than to please men.
What is needed is not the spirit but the Holy Spirit. What
the minister thinks of himself is of vital importance. He can
only win his place and have respect by a holy life.*[68]

May God be pleased to bring conviction to our hearts in this
most neglected area of discipline, for our good and his glory.

THE SPIRIT'S WORK IN PREACHING

While the Spirit's ministry is needed in every area of our lives
as pastors, it is especially needed in our preaching. Once again,
we see this in the preaching ministry of Paul, who reminded
the Corinthians: "My message and my preaching were not
in persuasive words of wisdom, but in demonstration of the
Spirit and of power, so that your faith would not rest on the
wisdom of men, but on the power of God" (1 Cor. 2:4-5). Paul
knew the profound importance of looking to the Holy Spirit for
instruction. We must do the same. Charles Spurgeon understood
this as well; commenting to his students, he said:

*The Spirit of God is peculiarly precious to us, because
he especially instructs us as to the person and work of
our Lord Jesus Christ; and that is the main point of our
preaching.... Let us wait upon the Spirit of God with this
cry—"O Holy Spirit, reveal to us the Son of God, and thus
show us the Father."*[69]

This is where we must begin in our prayers, earnestly
pleading with the Spirit for greater understanding, like the
psalmist who prayed: "Open my eyes, that I may behold
wonderful things from Your law (Ps. 119:18; cf. vv. 27, 34, 73, 125,
144, 169).

Various titles of the Holy Spirit found in Scripture provide wonderful insight into his unique role in our sanctification, including the instruction he gives in our sermon preparation, as well as the power he unleashes in our preaching. Here are four titles for your consideration:

1. BECAUSE HE IS "THE SPIRIT OF HOLINESS" (ROM. 4:1), THE HOLY SPIRIT MUST FIRST PREPARE THE HEART OF THE PREACHER.

Preparation for every sermon must start in the preacher's personal pursuit of holiness. This is where a man learns what Paul means to "discipline yourself for the purpose of godliness" (1 Tim. 4:7). This is where the man of God yields himself to the Spirit's control, seals out the cares of this world, and sets his affections on things above.

By devoting himself to the discipline of private piety, the faithful preacher learns to live in a *state of prayer* and *meditation upon the Word of life* in order to sustain and strengthen his soul. In the sacred closet of private worship, the Spirit speaks to the preacher's heart, reveals his sins, nourishes his soul, and brings Scripture to bear upon his life.

Samuel Davies (1723–1761) was a man known for his godliness; he was a Presbyterian preacher in colonial British America, one of the first non-Anglican preachers in Virginia, and one of the earliest missionaries to slaves in the British colonies. He succeeded Jonathan Edwards as President of Princeton University and helped lead the Southern phase of the religious revival known as the Great Awakening. Like many godly men of that era, he understood the importance of true communion with God and emphasized this as being more important than the technical aspects of preaching. Consider his persuasive words:

> *It is an easy thing to make a noise in the world, to flourish and harangue, to dazzle the crowd and set them all agape; but deeply to imbibe the Spirit of Christianity, to maintain a secret walk with God, to be holy, as he is holy—this is the labour, this is the work.*[70]

Similarly, John Witherspoon (1723–1794), a Scottish Presbyterian minister who was called to colonial British America to become the sixth president of Princeton University and ultimately a signatory to the July 4, 1776 *Declaration of Independence*, was also man with a passion for godliness. In his first sermon at Princeton, he affirmed as a certainty that "true religion in the heart is of far greater importance to the success and efficacy of the ministry than eminence or gifts."[71] He expanded upon this in his "Lectures on Eloquence" by listing "the qualities of most importance" for the preaching of the gospel, beginning with:

> *Piety—To have a firm belief of that gospel he is called to preach, and a lively sense of religion upon his own heart. . . . Precepts are often involved in obscurity, or warped by controversy; but a holy life immediately reaches, and takes possession of the heart . . . as the conclusion of the whole, that one devoted to the service of the gospel should be really, visibly, and eminently holy.*[72]

It was godly men like Samuel Davies, John Witherspoon, George Whitefield, Jonathan Edwards, and many others like them that God used to bring many to Christ during the first and second Great Awakening revivals in America. Imagine what God could do if every pastor had such a devotion to holiness.

We must understand, *personal piety is the fountainhead of a God-honoring sermon.* Therefore, preparation for Sunday's sermon is not merely what we do on Friday and Saturday, but is inextricably bound to *who we are* and *what we do* all week. Sermon preparation is a natural, inseparable part of the sanctifying work of the Spirit in our life that encompasses every moment we live. Every day the preacher must view what he experiences and reads through the lens of his text. Illustrations, examples, and additional insights will often appear in places he would least expect.

But all this begins with the Holy Spirit first preparing the heart of the preacher. When this happens, he will also discover the Spirit helping him prepare the actual sermon. Martyn Lloyd-Jones described it this way: "The preacher's first, and the most important task is to prepare himself, not his sermon."[73]

What a blessing it is to experience the intimate love of God at work, conforming us into the likeness of Christ, and accomplishing his good pleasure even in our preaching.

2. BECAUSE HE IS "THE SPIRIT OF WISDOM AND UNDERSTANDING, THE SPIRIT OF COUNSEL AND STRENGTH, THE SPIRIT OF KNOWLEDGE AND THE FEAR OF THE LORD" (ISAIAH 11:2), WE MUST CONTINUALLY SEEK HIS HELP IN THE COMBINED EFFORTS OF PREACHING AND SHEPHERDING.

The Holy Spirit has called and gifted his true shepherds to know the needs of their sheep and care for them accordingly. He has commanded them to "shepherd the flock of God ... with eagerness" (1 Peter 5:2). This primarily involves leading, feeding, and caring for those God has entrusted to us. Paul stated it clearly in his exhortation to the elders at Ephesus:

> *Be on guard for yourselves and for all the flock,*
> *among which the Holy Spirit has made you*
> *overseers, to shepherd the church of God which*
> *He purchased with His own blood. I know that*
> *after my departure savage wolves will come in*
> *among you, not sparing the flock; and from*
> *among your own selves men will arise, speaking*
> *perverse things, to draw away the disciples after*
> *them. Therefore be on the alert.*
>
> *(Acts 20:28-31)*

As we fellowship with our people, the Spirit makes us aware of their needs through a variety of ways and we must address them accordingly. The Shepherd of Psalm 23 serves as our example. The Spirit also brings these matters to mind in our preaching. But we must remember: *shepherding and preaching are far beyond our ability.* With Paul we say, "Who is adequate for these things?" (2 Cor. 2:16). Only the enabling ministry of the Spirit can make us vigilant in caring for our sheep through these inseparable duties.

As we implore the Holy Spirit for his supernatural assistance, he brings to light the great needs of his flock for us to see: those unique areas of sin that must be confronted, struggles that must be addressed, and sorrows that must be comforted. Then, with full understanding and confidence, we prepare our sermons and preach them with love and authority.

3. BECAUSE HE IS, "THE HELPER ... THE SPIRIT OF TRUTH WHO PROCEEDS FROM THE FATHER" WHO WILL "TESTIFY ABOUT [CHRIST]" (JOHN 15:26), WE MUST SEEK HIS INSTRUCTION IN UNDERSTANDING AND APPLYING HIS WORD.

Early in the week we must begin to meditate upon Sunday's text, seeking the help of the Spirit every day. Like a squirrel gathering nuts, we begin the process of gathering additional insights, illustrations, and quotations from our daily readings (which should be voracious). We also pay close attention to unique experiences we can use in our preparation and delivery. As we live in a state of prayerful communion, these provisions are laid in store, awaiting their proper application. Many will be used to help bridge the gap between the precise demands of exegesis and the final outline of the exposition.

But every step of the process must be done in a spirit of prayerful dependence upon "the Spirit of Truth" who enlightens our minds so that we can fully comprehend the full knowledge of God and his will (Eph. 1:17-18; Col. 1:9-10). Only then can we embrace, obey, and preach the truths he reveals (1 Cor. 2:10-16).

I am always amazed when I experience the Spirit's work in my heart and mind during the preparation and delivery of an exposition. Along with many other expositors, I have discovered that I never have to "come up with a sermon"; the Spirit always gives them to me. There has never been a time when I have had to frantically search for a text on Saturday to preach on Sunday, nor have I ever struggled during the week to find a topic. The texts are always waiting on me and the topics flow naturally from each passage when it is rightly divided.

This is always a work of the Spirit. And when this happens, my mind far outpaces my pen. I simply cannot write fast enough. I have to have a separate scratch sheet to jot down thoughts in shorthand so I can come back to them later. It is not uncommon to have them hit me out of the blue while doing something completely unrelated. With the Spirit's help, the original context, authorial intent, exegesis, and explanation of the passage become so abundantly clear that it is relatively easy to apply the passage to the contemporary issues of life.

And without fail, the ultimate and climactic theme of every exposition is the *glorious gospel of Jesus Christ*. Once again, the apostle Paul made this abundantly clear when he told the

Corinthians: "For I determined to know nothing among you except Jesus Christ, and Him crucified" (1 Cor. 2:2). This, of course, is no surprise, because the preparation has been supervised by the ministry of the Holy Spirit whom I have implored, the One Jesus promised to be, "the Helper . . . whom I will send to you from the Father, *that is* the Spirit of truth who proceeds from the Father, He will testify about Me" (John 15:26). Every Spirit-directed exposition will ultimately point to Jesus Christ.

Always preach the gospel! View every passage as another angle to gaze upon the beauty of Christ, like examining a magnificent diamond by turning it in every direction to see the countless shades of colors refracting through every crystal prism. The gospel is the diamond through which the Light of the World can be viewed in all the glory of his attributes (perfections), a tiny preview of what we will behold when we see him face-to-face.

4. FINALLY, BECAUSE THE HOLY SPIRIT "[CLOTHES US] WITH POWER FROM ON HIGH" (LUKE 24:49), WE MUST SEEK HIS BLESSING IN OUR SERMON DELIVERY, AND EXPECT IT.

The Spirit-filled preacher is a man who is continuously submitting to the Holy Spirit's control (Eph. 5:17-18). He will not only experience the Spirit's blessing in *preparation*, but also his empowerment in *proclamation*. Inevitably the Spirit will cause the text he studies to deeply impact his heart. If that fails to happen, something is terribly wrong! If a text does not move the preacher, how can he expect it to move his listeners? But oh, when it does, when the truth of divine grace erupts from the heart of a Spirit-empowered preacher, though the treasure is in an earthen vessel, the Word will go forth with such a supernatural force that neither man nor demon can stop it.

Charles Jefferson captures the very heart of a shepherd's work in these poignant words, a fitting summary to all that has been said concerning the convictions of a pastor's heart:

> *It is by no means easy for a young man to become a shepherd, and he ought not to be discouraged if he cannot become one in a day, or a year. An orator he can be without difficulty. A reformer he can become at once. In criticism of politics and society he can do a flourishing business the*

*first Sunday. But a shepherd he can become only slowly, and
by patiently traveling the way of the cross. The shepherd's
work is a humble work; such it has been from the beginning
and such it must be to the end. A man must come down to
it. A shepherd cannot shine. He cannot cut a figure. His
work must be done in obscurity. The things which he does
do not make interesting copy. His work calls for continuous
self-effacement. It is a form of service which eats up a man's
life. It makes a man old before his time. Every good shepherd
lays down his life for the sheep [be they 2 or thousands]. If
a man is dependent on the applause of the crowd, he ought
never to enter the ministry. The finest things a minister does
are done out of sight and never get reported. They are known
to himself, and to one or two others, and to God. His joy is
not that his success is being talked about on earth, but that
his name is written in heaven. The shepherd in the East had
no crowd to admire him. He lived alone with the sheep and
the stars. His satisfactions were from within. The messengers
of Christ must not expect bands of music to attend them on
their way. Theirs is humble, unpretentious, and oftentimes
unnoticed labor; but if it builds souls in righteousness
it is more lasting than the stars. . . . Nearness to Him is
the indispensable condition of absorbing the shepherd
temperament and learning the shepherd ways.*[74]

FINAL WORD

As a young man in the early 1970s, I enrolled in the Moody Bible
Institute in Chicago, Illinois. Though my spiritual immaturity
was far greater than I realized at that time, God graciously
began his loving, but often painful, process of pruning the
pitiful vine of my life, that I might one day bear more fruit for
his glory. That sanctifying process really began in one of the
first chapel services I attended. I do not remember the speaker,
but I do remember the story he told about D.L. Moody. While
in Dublin, Ireland, in 1873, after an all-night prayer meeting,
Moody heard British evangelist Henry Varley make an
offhanded statement that God used to change Moody's life. He
said, "The world has yet to see what God can do with and for

and through and in a man who is fully and wholly consecrated to Him."

Like Moody, I have never forgotten those words. Other than Jesus, perhaps the only man to meet the high standard was the apostle Paul. As we have seen over the course of our study, there were at least *seven key principles* that motivated and sustained him throughout his life, convictions that we as pastors and church leaders can apply to our hearts and allow to direct our lives and ministries as they did his. Paul was a man *consumed with God's glory, content with his suffering, convinced of his calling, controlled by one message, confident with one method, committed to one end,* and *confirmed by one power.*

May God use these principles to bless our lives and ministries, as together we serve the One who deserves our utmost. *Soli Deo Gloria!*

PRAISE TO THE LORD, THE ALMIGHTY

Praise to the Lord, the Almighty, the King of creation!
O my soul, praise him, for he is thy health and salvation!
All ye who hear,
Now to his temple draw near;
Join me in glad adoration!

Praise to the Lord, who o'er all things so wondrously reigneth,
Shelters thee under his wings, yea, so gently sustaineth!
Hast thou not seen
How thy desires all have been
Granted in what he ordaineth?

Praise to the Lord, who doth prosper thy work and defend thee;
Surely his goodness and mercy here daily attend thee.
Ponder anew
What the Almighty can do
If with his love he befriend thee.

Praise to the Lord! O let all that is in me adore him!
All that hath life and breath, come now with praises before him!
Let the "amen"
Sound from his people again;
Gladly forever adore him! Amen.

Joachim Neander (1650–1680)

ENDNOTES

1. C. H. Spurgeon, *Lectures to My Students* (Peabody, MA: Hendrickson Publishers Marketing, LLC, reprint of 1875 ed., Third Printing, 2012), 168.
2. David F. Wells, *God in the Wasteland* (Grand Rapids, MI: Eerdmans, 1994), 88.
3. Iain H. Murray, *The Forgotten Spurgeon*, (Edinburgh, The Banner of Trust, 1994), 40.
4. Excerpt from William Still's Sermon on John 20:10-18, from a recording at: http://tapesfromscotland.org/Audio3/3320.mp3
5. Paul David Tripp, *Awe*, (Wheaton, IL: Crossway, 2015), 50.
6. For an excellent biblical treatment on this subject, read Alexander Strauch's book: *Biblical Eldership: An Urgent Call to Restore Biblical Church Leadership*, Lewis and Roth Publishers.
7. George Whitefield, *The Method of Grace*, Sermon 58, from a recording at: http://anglicanlibrary.org/whitefield/sermons/58.htm
8. http://www.christianpost.com/news/the-dangerous-third-year-of-pastoral-tenure-121984/
9. John Calvin, *Institutes of the Christian Religion* (The Library of Christian Classics, Louisville, KY, Westminster John Knox Press, Reissued 2006), Chapter XVIII
10. C. H. Spurgeon, *Lectures to My Students* (Peabody, MA: Hendrickson Publishers Marketing, LLC, reprint of 1875 ed., Third Printing, 2012), 26.
11. Charles Bridges, *The Christian Ministry* (London: The Banner of Truth Trust, 1967, Reprint of 1830 ed.), 101.
12. Iain H. Murray, *Life of D. Martyn Lloyd-Jones*, Vol 2 (Edinburgh, The Banner of Truth Trust, Reprinted 2014), 429.
13. W. F. Arndt and F. W. Gingrich (trans. and ed.) of W. Bauer's *A Greek-English Lexicon of the New Testament and Other Early Christian Literature* (Chicago, IL: University of Chicago Press, Fourth Edition, 1952), 583.
14. George W. Knight, *The Pastoral Epistles: A Commentary on the Greek Text* (Grand Rapids, MI; Carlisle, England: William B. Eerdmans; Paternoster Press, 1992) 154.
15. Richard Baxter, *The Reformed Pastor* (Edinburgh: The Banner of Truth Trust, Reprinted 2005), 56.
16. Maurice Roberts, *The Thought of God* (Carlisle, PA: The Banner of Truth Trust, Reprinted 2013), 57.
17. Cited by I.D.E. Thomas, *Golden Treasury of Puritan Quotations* (Edinburgh: The Banner of Truth Trust,1975), 192.
18. C. H. Spurgeon, *Lectures to My Students* (Peabody, MA: Hendrickson Publishers Marketing, LLC, reprint of 1875 ed., Third Printing, 2012), 28.

19. In 2 Cor. 7:15 his fear and trembling was for the reverence of God and a healthy fear of judgment among the people. In Phil. 2:12-13 it was used to describe the proper attitude we should have toward offending God and the need to maintain a righteous awe of his holiness.

20. Quoted in John MacArthur, *The MacArthur New Testament Commentary: 1 Corinthians*: (Chicago, IL: Moody Press, 1984), 57.

21. This was most likely a false apostle in the church, inspired and empowered by Satan to pierce Paul's otherwise proud flesh with the thorn of slander—a divine remedy for arrogance.

22. John MacArthur, Jr. and the Master's Seminary Faculty, *Rediscovering Pastoral Ministry* (Nashville, TN: Word Publishing, 1995), 14-15.

23. Richard Baxter, *The Reformed Pastor* (Edinburgh: The Banner of Truth Trust, Reprint 2005), 178-179.

24. Jonathan Edwards, *The Works of Jonathan Edwards*, Vol 2 (Edinburgh: The Banner of Truth Trust), 183.

25. Ibid., 183

26. C. H. Spurgeon, *Lectures to My Students* (Peabody, MA: Hendrickson Publishers Marketing, LLC, reprint of 1875 ed., Third Printing, 2012), 28.

27. "Sola Scriptura" (Scripture Alone), "Sola Gratia" (Grace Alone), "Sola Fide" (Faith Alone), "Solus Christus" (Christ Alone), "Soli Deo Gloria" (To God Alone Be Glory)

28. http://www.pewforum.org/2017/08/31/u-s-protestants-are-not-defined-by-reformation-era-controversies-500-years-later/

29. Charles Spurgeon, *Election: Its Defenses and Evidences*, Sermon delivered in 1862.

30. https://www.barna.com/research/five-trends-among-the-unchurched/

31. Ibid.

32. John MacArthur and Richard Mayhue: General Editors, *Biblical Doctrine: A Systematic Summary of Bible Truth* (Wheaton, IL: Crossway, 2017), 924.

33. John MacArthur and the Master's Seminary faculty: *Rediscovering Expository Preaching* (Dallas, TX: Word Publishing, 1992), 348-349.

34. D. A. Carson, Gospel-Centered Ministry (Wheaton, IL: Crossway, 2011) by The Gospel Coalition / (Monergism).

35. David F. Wells, *The Courage to Be Protestant: Reformation Faith in Today's World, Second Edition* (Grand Rapids, MI: William B. Eerdmans Publishing Company, 2017), 9-10.

36. Ibid., 149.

37. John MacArthur, *The Gospel According to Jesus* (Nashville, TN: Nelson, 1993), 84.

38. Iain H. Murray, *The Life of Martyn Lloyd-Jones*, (Edinburgh: The Banner of Truth Trust, 2013), 130.

39. James Strong, *The New Strong's Expanded Exhaustive Concordance of the Bible* (Nashville, Thomas Nelson Publishers, 2001), 244.

40. G. C. Trench, *Synonyms of the New Testament* (Grand Rapids, MI: Eerdmans, 1973), 217–18.

41. James Strong, *The New Strong's Expanded Exhaustive Concordance of the Bible* (Nashville, Thomas Nelson Publishers, 2001), 162.

42. R. H. Mounce, *Romans* (Vol. 2). (Nashville, TN: Broadman & Holman Publishers, 1995), 232.
43. James Strong, *The New Strong's Expanded Exhaustive Concordance of the Bible* (Nashville, Thomas Nelson Publishers, 2001), 232.
44. Faris D. Whitesell, *Power in Expository Preaching* (Old Tappan, NJ: Revell, 1963), vi-viii.
45. John MacArthur and the Master's Seminary faculty, *Rediscovering Expository Preaching*, (Dallas, TX: Word Publishing, 1992).
46. D. Martyn Lloyd-Jones, *Preaching and Preachers* (Grand Rapids, MI: Zondervan, 1972).
47. C. H. Spurgeon, *Lectures to My Students* (Grand Rapids, MI: Baker Book House, Reprint 1977).
48. J. D. G. Dunn, *The Epistles to the Colossians and to Philemon: A commentary on the Greek Text* (Grand Rapids, MI; Carlisle: William B. Eerdmans Publishing; Paternoster Press, 1996), 125-6.
49. The concept of *perfections* is derived from the Greek term *aretas* ("excellencies"), the term Peter used in 1 Peter 2:9.
50. Cotton Mather, Student and Preacher, pp. iii-v, quoted by John R. W. Stott, *Between Two Worlds: The Art of Preaching in the Twentieth Century* (Grand Rapids, MI: William B. Eerdmans Publishing Co., Reprinted 2000), 31.
51. John Owen, *The Glory of Christ*, The Works of John Owen, Vol. 1, ed. William H. Goold, 1850 – 53, (Carlisle, PA: The Banner of Truth Trust, 1965), 460-461.
52. William Gurnall, *The Christian in Complete Armor*, (Peabody MA: Hendrickson Publishers, A reproduction of Blackie and Son [Scotland] edition, 1865), 416
53. *The MacArthur Topical Bible* (Nashville, TN: Word Publishing, 1999), 636-7.
54. Edward T. Welch, *The Journal of Biblical Counseling*, Volume 16, Number 3, Spring 1998, 25.
55. Bookman states: "The Hebrew verb translated 'observe' means 'to give themselves up to' or 'devote themselves to.' It suggests dogged determination or clinging to something in spite of influences to do otherwise. The lying vanity Jonah clung to was 'false love for his country, that he would not have his people go into captivity, when God would; would not have Nineveh preserved, the enemy of his country.' The phrase 'lying vanities' is more generic, it encompasses all things which man makes into idols or objects of trust." John F. MacArthur, Jr., Wayne A. Mack, and the Master's College Faculty, *Introduction to Biblical Counseling: A basic Guide to the Principles and Practice of Counseling* (Word Publishing, Dallas, London, Vancouver, Melbourne, 1994), 162.
56. The same is true with the current Same-Sex Attraction movement, which affirms that the Holy Spirit does not sanctify from unnatural affections.
57. Ibid., 164
58. Richard Baxter, *The Reformed Pastor* (Edinburgh: The Banner of Truth Trust, First published 1656, Reprinted 2005), 43.

59. Richard Baxter, *The Reformed Pastor* (Edinburgh: The Banner of Truth Trust, First published 1656, Reprinted 2005), 178-9.
60. J. D. G. Dunn, *The Epistles to the Colossians and to Philemon: A Commentary on the Greek T#ext* (Grand Rapids, MI; Carlisle: William B. Eerdmans Publishing; Paternoster Press: 1996), 126.
61. John Piper, *God's Passion For His Glory* (Wheaton, IL: Crossway Books, 1998), 43.
62. Jonathan Edwards, *The Most High A Prayer-Hearing God* (Sermon dated January, 1735-6 and 1752). (http://www.biblebb.com/files/edwards/prayer.htm)
63. Phillips Brooks, *The Joy of Preaching* (Grand Rapids, MI: Kregel, 1989), 47.
64. David Larsen, *The Anatomy of Preaching. Identifying the Issues in Preaching Today* (Grand Rapids, MI: Baker Book House, 1989), 53-54.
65. Richard Baxter, *The Reformed Pastor* (Edinburgh: The Banner of Truth Trust, Reprinted 2005), 74-75.
66. Copied for WholesomeWords.org from *Bright Examples: Short Sketches of Christian Life*. Dublin; London: Dublin Tract Repository, [1860] . . . https://www.wholesomewords.org/biography/bmcheyne8.html
67. Andrew A. Bonar, ed., *Memoirs of McCheyne* (Chicago, IL: Moody Publications, Reprinted 1978), 95.
68. Iain H. Murray, *The Life of Martyn Lloyd-Jones* (Edinburgh: The Banner of Truth Trust, 2013), 159.
69. C. H. Spurgeon, *Lectures to My Students*: (Peabody, MA: Hendrickson Publishers, Third Printing, 2012), 200.
70. Iain H. Murray, *Revival and Revivalism* (Edinburgh: The Banner of Truth Trust, 1994), 45.
71. Ibid., 45.
72. Ibid., 45-46.
73. D. Martyn Lloyd-Jones, *Preaching and Preachers* (Grand Rapids, MI: Zondervan Publishing House, 1971), 166.
74. Charles Jefferson, *The Minister As Shepherd; The Privileges and Responsibilities of Pastoral Leadership*, (Fort Washington, PA: CLC Publications, 2006), 27-28.

About Shepherd's Fire

Shepherd's Fire exists to proclaim the unsearchable riches of Christ through mass communications for the teaching ministry of Bible expositor Dr. David Harrell, with a special emphasis in encouraging and strengthening pastors and church leaders.

While the primary ministry media include the Internet, radio, private counseling, mentoring, seminars, and conferences, a new emphasis includes the development and publication of a range of mini-book resources, *The Compact Expository Pulpit Commentary Series*, addressing specific and often misunderstood doctrinal and practical issues. For more information see: www.shepherdsfire.org/mini-books.

Visit www.shepherdsfire.org to find out more about Shepherd's Fire.

Treasure in the Ashes:
Our Journey Home from the Ruins of Sexual Abuse

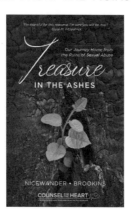

Sue Nicewander and Maria Brookins
Shepherd Press Trade Paperback, 368pp
ISBN: 978-1-63342-139-4

Treasure in the Ashes is an interactive book that gently leads readers on a biblical journey through the grueling questions and doubt, emotional turmoil, and relational fallout that follows sexual abuse.

Sue Nicewander, MABC, ACBC, BCC, has been counseling since 1994. She is founder and training coordinator of Biblical Counseling Ministries, Wisconsin Rapids, Wisconsin, and serves on the Council Board of the Biblical Counseling Coalition. Sue has her MA in biblical counseling from Central Baptist Theological Seminary. Sue and her late husband Jim were married for 43 years. The Nicewander family includes two beautiful married daughters and six delightful grandchildren.

Maria Brookins has a BS in Biblical Studies/Counseling from Faith Baptist Bible College in Ankeny, Iowa. She and her husband, Corey, have been serving together in ministry since 2004. They enjoy God's gift of a full and vibrant life with four fabulous boys and two crazy dogs.

"I'm thankful for this resource. I'm sure you will be, too."
—*Elyse M. Fitzpatrick*

"I pray this book finds its way into the hands of everyone who has undergone the wretched experience of sexual abuse."
—*Curtis W. Solomon*

DISCIPLING THE FLOCK:
A CALL TO FAITHFUL SHEPHERDING

Paul Tautges
Shepherd Press Trade Paperback, 96pp
ISBN: 978-1-63342-142-4

Here is an urgent appeal to return to authentic discipleship; here is a call to shepherds to be tenacious in their preaching of the whole counsel of God, and tender in their application of its truth to the lives of God's sheep through personal ministry.

Author Paul Tautges has been in gospel ministry since 1992 and currently serves as senior pastor of Cornerstone Community Church (EFCA) in Cleveland, Ohio. Paul is the author of many books including *Comfort the Grieving*, *Counseling One Another*, and *Pray about Everything*, and serves as the series editor for the LifeLine mini-books. He is also an adjunct professor and blogs at CounselingOneAnother.com.

"Here is an anchor for authentic ministry that will stimulate real spiritual growth in God's people." —Dr. Steven J. Lawson

"... this book gets it right." —John MacArthur

"...a biblically faithful, practically helpful guide to find the important balance between the public and private ministry of the Word of God..."

—Brian Croft, Senior Pastor,
Auburndale Baptist Church, Louisville, Kentucky

COUNSEL WITH CONFIDENCE:
A QUICK REFERENCE GUIDE
FOR BIBLICAL COUNSELORS AND DISCIPLERS

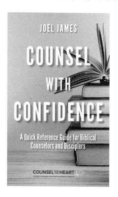

Joel James
Shepherd Press Trade paperback, 224pp
ISBN: 978-1-63342-148-6

When you were learning to ride a bicycle, the hardest part was the first few pedal strokes—those wobbly seconds before you built up enough momentum to maintain your balance. A generous push from your dad was just what you needed to avoid ending up in a heap of elbows, knees, handlebars, and spokes. Counseling is similar. Sometimes you need something to give you some momentum, something to give you the confidence that you're on the right track. If you've ever felt like that, this book is for you.

Author Joel James has an M.Div. and a D.Min. from The Master's Seminary and is the pastor-teacher of Grace Fellowship in Pretoria, South Africa. He and his wife, Ruth, have been married since 1993 and have two children.

"The book's concise entries are time-saving, insightful, biblical, and practical, which make this reference guide a must-have for any bookshelf."

—John MacArthur

"Read and use this book with help and profit. You'll be grateful you did."

—Lance Quinn

COUNSELING ONE ANOTHER:
A THEOLOGY OF INTERPERSONAL DISCIPLESHIP

Paul Tautges
Trade paperback, 192pp
ISBN: 978-1-63342-094-6

A book to help believers understand the process of being transformed by
God's grace and truth

"This book gets it right! Comprehensive and convincing, Counseling
One Another *shows how true biblical counseling and preaching fit
hand-in-glove. Those who preach, teach or counsel regularly are sure to
benefit greatly from this helpful resource."*
—*Dr. John MacArthur, Pastor-Teacher,*
Grace Community Church;
President, The Master's University and Seminary

*"Paul Tautges lays the theological foundation for biblical counseling—
in a way that is both comprehensive and compassionate. This book
demonstrates a staunch commitment to an expository, exegetical
examination of counseling as presented in God's Word. Any pastor or
lay person wanting a foundational starting point for understanding
Christ-centered, comprehensive, and compassionate biblical counseling
in the local church would be wise to read and reread* Counseling
One Another.*"*
—*Bob Kellemen,*
Executive Director of The Biblical Counseling Coalition

About Shepherd Press Publications

- They are gospel driven.
- They are heart focused.
- They are life changing.

Our Invitation to You

We passionately believe that what we are publishing can be of benefit to you, your family, your friends, and your work colleagues. So we are inviting you to join our online mailing list so that we may reach out to you with news about our latest and forthcoming publications, and with special offers. Visit:

www.shepherdpress.com/newsletter

and provide your name and email address.